Women Scientists and Inventors
A Science Puzzle Book

Jacquelyn A. Greenblatt
Illustrated by Corasue Nicholas

Good Year Books

An Imprint of Addison-Wesley Educational Publishers, Inc.

Good Year Books

are available for most basic curriculum subjects plus many enrichment areas. For more Good Year Books, contact your local bookseller or educational dealer. For a complete catalog with information about other Good Year Books, Please write:

Good Year Books

Scott Foresman-Addison Wesley
1900 East Lake avenue
Glenview, IL 60025

Book design by Ann Rebidas.
Copyright © 1999 Good Year Books, an imprint of Addison-Wesley Educational Publishers Inc.
All Rights Reserved.
Printed in the United States of America.

ISBN 0-673-57728-7

2 3 4 5 6 7 8 9 – ML – 02 01 00 99

 This Book Is Printed on Recycled Paper

CONTENTS

INTRODUCTION

This book contains puzzles that are fun and challenging. At the same time, it should help elementary and middle school students expand their vocabularies and improve reading comprehension. Each of the 42 puzzles consists of two parts. First, a short narrative describes and explains a discovery made by a female scientist or inventor. This text is followed by a puzzle that, when solved, reveals the name of the woman responsible for the accomplishment.

The female scientists and inventors included in this book were selected on the basis of the creativity and conceptual innovation of their work. Much still remains to be learned about the role of women in the history of science. Yet, even with the limited material presently available, women from nearly every important scientific area—mathematics, physics, chemistry, biology, and applied science—have been included. As examples of the scientific capabilities of women, these female scientists should be inspirational to both girls and boys.

The vocabulary used in the puzzles was dictated in part by the nature of the scientific discoveries. But the vocabulary was selected as much as possible for its suitability to students in the higher grades of elementary school and in middle school.

All words needed to solve each puzzle are found either in the puzzle itself or, more often, in the text that precedes it. Therefore, a careful reading of the narrative is essential before a student attempts to solve a puzzle. If this is done and a student still experiences difficulty with any question, the student should simply refer back to the text. In the more difficult puzzles, some letters of the missing words are provided as clues. Solutions to the puzzles appear at the end of the book.

Once students have completed all of the puzzles, they will have been introduced to hundreds of vocabulary words. Students will also become acquainted with varied scientific ideas and little-known biographical information about important women scientists and inventors. This knowledge should lead to better performance in school. Equally important, students will acquire new vocabulary and basic concepts necessary for learning in future years.

Curing Diseases: Forty-Five Patents and a Nobel Prize

Have you heard about a person who recovered from leukemia? Do you know someone who received a successful kidney transplant with the help of immunosuppressant drugs, medicines that decrease the effectiveness of the body's immune system? Credit for these modern scientific "miracles" goes in large part to an ingenious American-born and educated female biochemist. Working between 1944 and the early 1980s, she developed and patented a total of forty-five medications. Her investigations involved not only leukemia and the rejection of transplanted organs, but also gout, malaria, and herpes.

As part of her efforts, this biochemist carefully observed the differences between the workings of normal human cells and the functioning of cancer cells and pathogenic or disease-producing organisms. These harmful organisms include bacteria, viruses, and microscopic animals called protozoa. Then she developed drugs that did not harm normal human body cells, but killed or interfered with the way cancer cells and pathogenic organisms grow and reproduce. This new approach to developing medicines has prevented numerous epidemics and deaths. In recognition of her achievements, this female biochemist, along with her associate, George Hitchings, received the 1988 Nobel Prize for Physiology or Medicine.

To find this woman biochemist's name, complete the crossword tree on the next page. Use the clues provided. All the words you need are included in the text above.

Puzzle 1   Curing Diseases: Forty-Five Patents and a Nobel Prize

									¹	O	W		
²M	E	D		C									
							³	E	C		V	E	R
⁴B	I		C	H		I	S						
						⁵	E				U	C	E
				⁶E									
					⁷	E		T	H				
⁸D	I	S		S									
				⁹	P		D	E	M		C		
		¹⁰C	E										
				¹¹	T	E		F	E	R			
¹²I		M		N									
				¹³	O	R		A	L				

Across

1. Increase in size; develop toward maturity
2. Drug or other substance used to treat disease
3. Regain health
4. Scientist who deals with chemistry of life processes
5. Produce others of one's own kind
6. First three letters of word meaning "trained" or "schooled"
7. Ending of life
8. Illness
9. Rapid spread of sickness
10. Basic structural and functional unit of living things
11. Oppose; come between for some purpose
12. Prefix meaning immune or immunity
13. Usual; average

Down

1. Female biochemist who received the 1988 Nobel Prize for Physiology or Medicine

The First Computer Programmer

Nowadays, many people are computer programmers, persons who create coded instructions that tell computers which operations to perform to solve a problem or to process information. But who was the first computer programmer?

The answer goes back to the mid-1830s. At that time, the English mathematician, Charles Babbage, drew up detailed plans for an "analytical engine," a new kind of calculating machine. This proposed machine was actually an early computer since the analytical engine was designed to contain punch cards. The position of the holes in these cards would be interpreted as numerical data and operating instructions by the analytical engine.

In 1840 at the University of Turin in Italy, Babbage lectured on his plans for the analytic engine. These lectures were eventually published in French, and in 1843 a British female mathematician agreed to translate the lectures into English.

However, this woman mathematician did more than just study the lectures briefly, absorb Babbage's ideas, and then translate his work. Although she did not redo his lectures, during the course of a year, she added her own notes consisting of comments and explanations. These notes tripled the length of Babbage's lectures and aided in the understanding of his analytical engine. For example, in one of these notes she explained how to use the punch cards to write a program for the analytical engine. In another note, she actually wrote out a program.

Unfortunately, Babbage was unable to obtain financing and the analytical engine was never built. But in 1855, a Swedish firm produced a calculator incorporating some of his ideas.

Discover the name of the first computer programmer by completing the word links on the next page. In these links, the last letter of one word becomes the first letter of the next. All words can be found in the text above. After you have completed the puzzle, write, in order, the numbered first letter of each word.

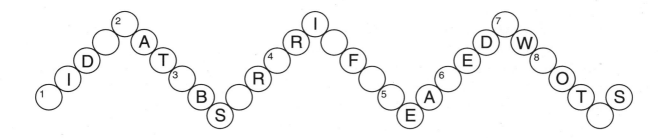

Puzzle 2 The First Computer Programmer

I D A T B S R R I F E A E D W O T S

1. Helped; assisted
2. Information
3. Take in; suck up
4. Concisely
5. 365 days
6. Do again; do over
7. Belonging or relating to oneself
8. Comments or explanations, frequently at the bottom of a page

__ __ __   __ __ __ __ __
 1 2 3   4 5 6 7 8

Women Scientists and Inventors **5**

Saving Blue Babies

Before the middle of the twentieth century, one of the saddest sights in hospitals was small children with heart problems. These children often had a bluish tint to their skin and, as a result, were called "blue babies."

In the 1930s an American female pediatrician examining heart X rays discovered a series of internal structural defects in the hearts of these children. The defects included an opening in the wall between the two major heart chambers, an improperly working heart valve, and partial blockage of the artery leading from the heart to the lungs. An artery is a blood vessel that carries blood away from the heart.

Because of these defects, some of the blood returning to the right side of the heart from the body was pumped back into circulation without first going to the lungs. Since the lungs are the place where blood acquires oxygen, the blood failed to get all of the oxygen needed. This lack of oxygen caused the children to feel weak. Another effect was the bluish tinge to the skin, an indication that the blood underneath did not have enough oxygen.

Determined to help, this female pediatrician designed new surgical procedures. In one procedure, she joined two formerly separate arteries in order to bypass the problem area in the heart. The surgery was successful and the goal of carrying more blood to the lungs was achieved. Today, blue babies no longer face a negative future. Instead, they undergo surgery and then lead normal, active lives.

To find the name of this creative pediatric heart specialist, solve the puzzle on the next page by writing the correct word next to its definition. Use the words in the word box. All words can be found in the above text. After you have written the correct words, write the first letter of each word above its number at the bottom of the page.

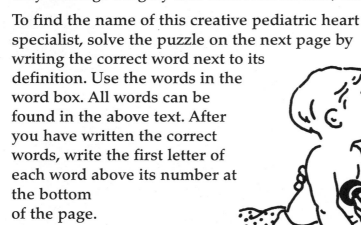

Name _____ Date _____

Puzzle 3 Saving Blue Babies

artery	effect	examine	goal	heart	internal
lung	negative	structural	surgery	tinge	underneath

1. Body organ that pumps blood

1. _____

2. Consequence; result

2. _____

3. Body organ where oxygen is acquired

3. _____

4. Inspect

4. _____

5. Opposite of *positive*

5. _____

6. Slight coloring

6. _____

7. Blood vessel that carries blood away from the heart

7. _____

8. Below

8. _____

9. Relating to the way parts are constructed

9. _____

10. Medical operation

10. _____

11. Occurring inside

11. _____

12. Objective

12. _____

__ __ __ __ __   __ __ __ __ __ __ __
1 2 3 4 5   6 7 8 9 10 11 12

Formulas for Einstein

When Albert Einstein presented his revolutionary theory of relativity in 1905, the world was awed by its scope and originality. In an orderly fashion, this theory explained several complex subjects relating to the universe and the Earth and included the concept that matter and energy are equivalent.

Yet, as convincing as Einstein's explanations seemed, scientists could accept his theory only if it proved in agreement with accepted laws of physics. If inconsistencies or disagreements were found, either Einstein's theory or the accepted laws would have to be modified.

Among the accepted laws of physics are the laws of conservation of energy. The principle of conservation of energy states that energy can neither be created nor destroyed; it can only change in form. For example, an automobile engine changes the chemical energy of gasoline into motion energy and heat energy. But the total amount of energy in the system remains the same.

Initially, some physicists claimed that Einstein's theory was inconsistent with this principle. A female mathematician working in Germany between 1908 and 1919 responded to these claims. She not only used specific numbers but also devised general mathematical formulas showing that Einstein's theory is in agreement with the principle of conservation of energy. In this way, she overcame a major hurdle to the theory's acceptance.

Dismissed from her teaching position in Germany when the Nazis came to power, this theoretical mathematician immigrated to the United States. She then taught at Bryn Mawr and Princeton.

To find the name of this remarkable woman who used mathematics to bolster the theory of relativity, unscramble each jumbled word (on the next page) and write the correct word next to it. All correctly written words appear in the text above. After you have unscrambled the words, write the first letter of each word above its number at the bottom of the page.

Puzzle 4   Formulas for Einstein

1. TEESININ   __ __ N __ __ E I N

2. STAMTHECIAM   __ A __ H __ M __ T I C __

3. TATREM   __ A __ T E R

4. TEY   __ __ T

5. RENBUM   __ U M __ E R

6. REDYROL   __ R __ E __ L Y

7. YERNEG   __ N __ __ G Y

8. YORETH   __ H __ __ R Y

9. HELDRU   __ U R __ L E

10. RETHA   __ A __ T H

11. VITALYRITE   __ E L __ __ I V __ __ Y

1. Originator of the theory of relativity
2. Science that uses numbers and symbols to deal with quantities
3. Substance; material
4. However; nevertheless
5. Symbol or word telling how many
6. Systematic; neat in arrangement
7. Capacity for doing work
8. Statement of apparent underlying principles based on observation
9. Obstacle; difficulty
10. Our planet
11. Einstein's theory, presented in 1905

__ __ __ __   __ __ __ __ __ __ __
1 2 3 4   5 6 7 8 9 10 11

The Spiral Shape of DNA

Frequently newspapers announce that scientists have identified a new gene, the basic unit of hereditary matter. Each of these new genes is claimed to be linked to a particular disease, such as cancer or diabetes, or to a specific trait, such as height or weight.

The groundwork for these amazing findings was laid in the middle of the twentieth century when scientists determined the structure of the DNA molecule, the major component of genes. A molecule consists of two or more atoms. Atoms are the smallest particle of an element, which is a substance that cannot be broken down into a simpler substance by chemical means.

This breakthrough discovery of the structure of DNA is attributed to Francis Crick and Maurice Wilkins of Great Britain and James Watson of the United States. In recognition of their work, they received the Nobel Prize for Physiology or Medicine in 1962. Crick, Wilkins, and Watson had developed a double helix model of the DNA molecule. This model consisted of two spirals made up of chains of atoms wound around each other like a twisted ladder. These spirals separate and make copies of themselves during cell reproduction.

In the 1950s, before Crick and Wilkins won their award, a British female biophysicist had studied images produced by passing X rays through DNA. This process is called X-ray diffraction. Using this process, this biophysicist had determined the density of DNA and concluded that the DNA molecule is spiral-shaped. However, she did not suggest two intertwined spirals. Crick, Wilkins, and Watson, in constructing their prize-winning model, based their work partly on her data.

To find the name of this unheralded British biophysicist, solve the puzzle on the next page. First circle one letter in each box from left to right to make one 5-letter word, two 4-letter words, and one 3-letter word. Use the clues to help find the words in the text above. After you have circled the correct letters, start at the top and write the uncircled letters from left to right on the spaces at the bottom of the page.

Puzzle 5   The Spiral Shape of DNA

1.	HR	OE	SL	IA	LX
2.	IG	EN	DN	FE
3.	RX	AR	AN	KY
4.	DL	IN	NA

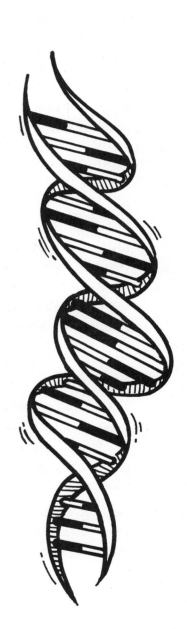

1. Spiral
2. Hereditary unit occurring at specific points on a chromosome
3. Type of short-wave radiation that can produce images on photographic plates
4. Abbreviation for name of the molecule that is the major component of genes

_ _ _ _ _ _ _ _ _   _ _ _ _ _ _ _

The Atomic Nature of Radioactivity

In 1895 a French physicist named Antoine Becquerel discovered that uranium compounds emit radiation as high-energy rays. A Polish-born woman, then living in France, was fascinated by this discovery. She already had degrees in physics and mathematics and decided that for her graduate work she would investigate this radiation.

Her studies revealed that the magnitude, or amount, of radiation depended on the quantity of uranium in the compounds. The amount of radiation was unaffected by the type of uranium compound or by temperature or light. She therefore suggested that radiation is an atomic property caused by activity within the atom's nucleus, the central part of the atom where particles called protons and neutrons are located. In 1898 she made up the word *radioactivity* to describe this activity.

During her experiments, this woman scientist and her husband tested pitchblende, an ore of uranium. She found that the radioactivity of the pitchblende was far greater than she had expected based on the quantity of uranium in the ore. As a result, she proposed that the pitchblende contained an element even more radioactive than uranium. Eventually, she isolated or separated two new radioactive elements, polonium and radium, from the pitchblende.

For her work on radioactivity, this woman scientist, along with her husband and Antoine Becquerel, received the Nobel Prize for Physics in 1903. For her discovery of polonium and radium and the isolation of radium from pitchblende, she alone received the Nobel Prize for Chemistry in 1911.

To find the name of this female scientist, write the correct word next to each clue on the next page. All answers appear in the text above. After you have written the correct words, write the first letter of each word above its number at the bottom of the page.

Puzzle 6   The Atomic Nature of Radioactivity

1. Size; amount   _ A G _ _ T U D _

2. Relating to atoms   _ _ _ _ M I C

3. High-energy rays   _ A D _ _ _ _ I O N

4. Separate; set apart from others   _ S O _ _ T E

5. Substance that cannot be separated into
   different substances by ordinary chemical methods _ L E _ _ N T

6. Science that deals with the composition and
   properties of substances   _ _ E _ I S _ R Y

7. Radioactive element studied by Becquerel   _ R A _ _ U M

8. Radioactive element found in pitchblende   _ _ D _ U M

9. Inquire into; study   _ _ V E S _ I _ A T E

10. Procedure to test a possible explanation   _ _ P E R _ _ E N T

_ _ _ _ _   _ _ _ _ _
1 2 3 4 5   6 7 8 9 10

Radial Tires and Bulletproof Vests

In 1965 an American female chemist working at DuPont Corporation laboratories did indeed invent the substance used in tires and bulletproof vests. Kevlar is DuPont's name for the tough, rigid fiber that is an important part of such objects as radial tires, helmets, bulletproof vests, airplanes, space vehicles, skis, sails, and boat shells.

A graduate of Carnegie Institute of Technology, this woman chemist joined DuPont in 1946 in order to earn money to attend medical school. At DuPont, she worked on chaining together simple molecules to form longer, more complex molecules called polymers. These polymers had new properties and formed the basis of many human-made fibers, including nylon. Her work proved so interesting that she never left for medical school.

One of this woman chemist's objectives at DuPont was to develop strong and stable polymers. In her experiments, she used liquid solutions containing crystals that dissolved at low heat and could be spun into fibers at room temperature. One such solution yielded exceptionally tough fibers that were even stronger than steel. These fibers formed the basis of Kevlar. By the time she retired from DuPont in 1986, she had 17 different patents.

To find this woman chemist's name, circle the one word that doesn't belong in each row of words on the next page. Then, starting with row 1, write the first letter of each circled word on the blanks at the bottom of the page.

Puzzle 7   Radial Tires and Bulletproof Vests

1.	complicated	complex	simple	elaborate
2.	property	temperature	trait	characteristic
3.	nylon	experiment	polyester	Kevlar
4.	stable	fixed	polymer	enduring
5.	heat	strong	durable	tough
6.	dissolve	melt	liquefy	airplane
7.	artificial	natural	counterfeit	synthetic
8.	objective	goal	invent	aim
9.	equation	basis	foundation	support
10.	rigid	inflexible	stiff	key
11.	produce	yield	ways	furnish
12.	link	ore	chain	connect
13.	liquid	make	form	fashion
14.	patent	trademark	copyright	environment
15.	mixture	combination	solution	know

___ ___ ___ ___ ___ ___ ___ ___ ___   ___ ___ ___ ___ ___ ___
1   2   3   4   5   6   7   8   9   10 11 12 13 14 15

The Modern Street-Cleaning Machine

Every day huge street-cleaning trucks lumber down city streets. These trucks spray fine mists of water onto the street. The mists loosen the dirt and litter so that the huge brushes can sweep them into the trucks. But few persons are aware that the first such street-cleaning device was created around 1900 by a New York woman.

In her former career as a journalist, this female inventor had watched giant presses print, fold, count, and bind newspapers. Her original street-cleaning machine applied the same criteria, or standards: one machine should perform several tasks in an efficient manner. Thus, the driver of an enclosed horse-drawn wagon pressed a foot pedal that released a spray of water that moistened street dirt. Then a large, rotating broom attached to the wagon gathered the trash and pushed it up a ramp into the wagon. There, protected from being scattered by the wind, the waste was compressed.

To find the name of this woman inventor of the first modern street-cleaning machine, complete the crossword tree on the next page. Use the clues provided. All the words you need are included in the text above.

Puzzle 8   The Modern Street-Cleaning Machine

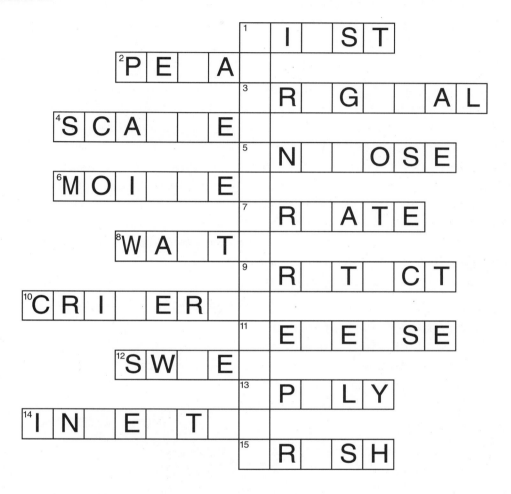

¹	I		S	T		
²P	E	A				
³	R		G		A	L
⁴S	C	A		E		
⁵	N		O	S	E	
⁶M	O	I		E		
⁷	R		A	T	E	
⁸W	A		T			
⁹	R		T		C	T
¹⁰C	R	I	E	R		
¹¹	E		E		S	E
¹²S	W	E				
¹³	P		L	Y		
¹⁴I	N		E	T		
¹⁵	R		S	H		

Across

1. Ranking before all others in a series
2. Lever operated by the foot
3. Earliest one of a type; that from which copies are made
4. Separate and go off in different directions
5. Shut in on all sides; fence in
6. Dampen
7. Bring into existence; make
8. Discarded material
9. Shield from loss or harm
10. Standards by which something is judged
11. Set free from confinement; let loose
12. Clear away dirt with a broom
13. Put to some practical or specific use
14. Originator of a new device
15. Rubbish

Down

1. Inventor of the first modern street-cleaning machine

The Origin of the Elements

How did the many elements on Earth originate? Did common elements such as carbon and oxygen form in the same manner as rare elements like rhenium and xenon? Was the creation of the elements a random occurrence or was it a predictable happening?

In the 1950s, an English female astronomer trying to answer these questions studied the wavelengths of light emitted by stars. Relying on carefully gathered data, she developed a theory to help understand the origin of the elements. Her theory states that as a star ages over long periods of time, most elements are born through the process of nuclear fusion. Nuclear fusion is the binding together of lighter elements to form progressively heavier ones. As fusion occurs, a star's mass becomes denser. The star's gravitational pull, or attraction for other matter, is also greater. Eventually the largest stars collapse inward. An explosive outward rebound follows, during which the heaviest elements are created.

This theory came to be known as the B2FH theory in honor of the female astronomer who formulated it and the other scientists who collaborated with her: her husband Geoffrey, William Fowler, and Sir Fred Hoyle. Other scientists have tried without success to rebut, or disprove, this theory.

To find the female originator of the B2FH theory, solve the puzzle on the next page. On each line, write the opposite of the word or group of words on the left. All answers appear in the word box and in the text above. After you have written all the correct answers, write the first letter of each answer above its number on the lines at the bottom of the page.

Puzzle 9   The Origin of the Elements

age	astronomer	bind	born	denser	emit
explosive	gather	gravitation	inward	mass	
rare	rebut	rely	together	understand	

1. Emptiness; void

2. Geologist

3. Confirm

4. Scatter

5. Grow younger

6. Distrust

7. Take in; absorb

8. Alone

9. Died

10. Comprehend incorrectly

11. Plentiful; common

12. Come apart; disintegrate

13. Toward the outside

14. More spread out

15. Repulsion

16. Calm and quiet

1. _____

2. _____

3. _____

4. _____

5. _____

6. _____

7. _____

8. _____

9. _____

10. _____

11. _____

12. _____

13. _____

14. _____

15. _____

16. _____

__ __ __ __ __ __ __ __   __ __ __ __ __ __ __ __
1 2 3 4 5 6 7 8   9 10 11 12 13 14 15 16

Jumping Genes

In the second half of the nineteenth century, an Austrian monk named Gregor Mendel grew pea plants through several generations. He discovered that inherited traits such as height and color are determined by factors that act as distinct units. Later, biologists called these units genes. Biologists are specialists in the study of living things. From the evidence they had, biologists assumed that genes were small, simple, fixed amounts of hereditary material strung together in a set order like beads on threadlike strands called chromosomes.

But in 1951, a female American botanist reported that this assumption was inconsistent with what she had observed in her experiments. She had been studying maize kernels for seven years in a laboratory in Cold Spring Harbor, New York. Maize kernels are seeds of corn. She had discovered that certain genes that act as switches and control the activity of other genes transfer, or jump, from one chromosome to another. The timing of these movements appeared to be related to the stage of development of the maize plants.

Many of this botanist's colleagues at first rejected the concept of "jumping genes" that regulate other genes. However, molecular biologists in the 1970s verified her finding through new experiments. Molecular biologists study the chemical and physical principles relating to molecules in living cells. In 1983 this female biologist, who had studied maize kernels so carefully, received the Nobel Prize for Physiology or Medicine for her work. She was the first woman honored with an unshared award in this category.

To find the name of the discoverer of jumping genes, write the correct word next to each clue on the next page. All answers appear in the text above. After you have written all the correct words, write the first letter of each word above its number under the clues.

Puzzle 10   Jumping Genes

1. Specialist in the study of plants   _ O T _ _ _ S T

2. Prize   _ W _ R D

3. Refuse to accept; discard   _ E _ E C T

4. Specialist in the study of living things   _ I O _ _ G _ S T

5. Take for granted as a fact   _ _ _ U M E

6. Give information about or write an account of something seen or done   _ _ _ _ O R T

7. Normal function of a body   _ _ _ I V _ T Y

8. Corn   _ A _ Z E

9. Threadlike strand that carries genes   _ H _ O _ O S _ M E

10. Idea; abstract notion   _ _ _ _ C E P _

11. Room or building for scientific experimentation or research   _ _ B O R _ _ _ R Y

12. Receive from an ancestor   _ N _ E _ I T

13. Ordinal number preceded by eighteen others in a series   _ I N _ _ E E _ T H

14. Move or send from one place to another   _ R A N _ _ E R

15. Sequence in which things are arranged   _ R _ E R

16. Exercise power over   _ O _ T _ O L

17. Grain or seed of corn   _ E R _ E L

— — — — — — —   — — — — — — — — — —
1 2 3 4 5 6 7   8 9 10 11 12 13 14 15 16 17

The Discovery of Pulsars

In 1967 a British female graduate student studying astronomy at Cambridge University in England detected unusual but regularly patterned radio signals, or pulses, on the observatory's radio telescope. A radiotelescope uses an antenna or group of antennae to receive and measure radio waves from space instead of using lenses that focus light rays. This female graduate student and Anthony Hewish, director of her astronomy project, determined that the time between bursts of energy was always exactly the same—just over a second. Later, these two astronomers concluded that the signals were radio energy from a dense, rapidly rotating star, composed almost entirely of neutrons, one of the basic particles in the atom.

Other such stars, each six miles or less in diameter, were soon located. The length of the time between pulses varied, depending upon the star. But for each individual star the time between pulses was always exactly the same, or uniform. The stars were given the name pulsating radio stars or pulsars, for short.

Astronomers believe that pulsars are formed when the core of a supernova collapses inward. A supernova is an extremely bright nova, a star that suddenly increases in brightness, or luminosity, and then decreases in brightness over a longer period of time. The neutrons at the surface of this compressed star change into protons and electrons. Neutrons have no charge, but protons have a positive charge and electrons have an equal but negative charge. The charged particles enter the magnetic field that surrounds the star and rotate with it. Energy radiating from these particles is detected on Earth as pulses.

For the identification of this entirely new class of stars, Anthony Hewish and Sir Martin Ryle, the leader of Cambridge University's radio astronomy group, jointly received the 1974 Nobel Prize for Physics. Not included among the recipients was the youthful woman graduate student who had discovered the first pulsar.

You can find her name, however, by unscrambling each jumbled word (on the next page) and writing the correct word next to it. Use the clues below the words. All correctly written words appear in the text above. After you have unscrambled the words, write the first letter of each word above its number at the bottom of the page.

Name _____ Date _____

Puzzle 11   The Discovery of Pulsars

1. TIJON   _ O _ N T   8. SURBT   _ U _ S T

2. TORRYVASBOE _ B _ E _ V _ T _ R Y   9. MUNRIFO   _ _ _ F O R _

3. SALCS   _ L _ S S   10. ARTOTE   _ O _ A T E

4. CELTNORE   _ _ E C _ _ O N   11. VOAN   _ O V _

5. SNEL   _ E N _   12. LEERYNIT   _ N T I _ _ L Y

6. FOUTHULY   _ O U _ _ F U L   13. YUMSLINITO _ U M _ _ O S _ T Y

7. RONNUTE   _ E U _ _ O N   14. GNELTH   _ E N _ T H

1. Common to or shared by two or more persons
2. Building equipped with large telescope for astronomical research
3. Category
4. Atomic particle with a negative charge
5. Transparent substance with one or two curved surfaces used to direct light passing through it
6. Young
7. Type of atomic particle most common in pulsars
8. Spurt; sudden forceful action
9. Exactly the same
10. Turn around a center point
11. Star whose brightness suddenly increases and then more slowly decreases
12. Completely
13. Brightness
14. Extent in time; measure of anything from end to end

__ __ __ __ __ __ __   __ __ __ __ __ __ __
1 2 3 4 5 6 7   8 9 10 11 12 13 14

Sunspots, Jupiter's Surface, and Saturn's Rings

Sunspots, dark dots on the sun's otherwise brilliant surface, have intrigued astronomers for hundreds of years. In the early seventeenth century, Galileo observed sunspots through his telescopes. He concluded that sunspots are features on the sun's surface. But lacking detailed images, he was not more specific.

However, in the middle of the nineteenth century, an American female astronomer who already had studied solar eclipses took daily pictures of sunspots. This woman astronomer carefully inspected her photos of sunspots and concluded that they are vast, circular, quick-moving, tornadolike masses of whirling gas that reach great heights. Scientists still hold this view today.

This American female astronomer also studied Jupiter's moons and Jupiter's surface, which is hidden by clouds. She asserted that Jupiter is composed entirely of clouds. No solid surface, level or mountainous, exists beneath the atmosphere. This view was not shared by most astronomers of her time, but it is now widely accepted.

In addition, this original-thinking astronomer focused her attention on multiringed Saturn. She noted that the light reflected by Saturn is different in appearance from the light reflected by its rings. Her interpretation of this observation was that the planet and its rings are composed of different materials. Later astronomical data supported this explanation.

To find the name of this nineteenth-century woman responsible for these new astronomical ideas, write the correct word next to its definition on the next page. All words can be found in the word box and in the text above. After you have written all the correct words, write the first letter of each word above its number at the bottom of the page.

Puzzle 12   Sunspots, Jupiter's Surface, and Saturn's Rings

astronomical	atmosphere	circular	eclipse	height	image
inspect	level	light	circular	material	eclipse	moon	ring	tornado

astronomical   atmosphere   circular   eclipse   height   image
inspect   level   light   material   moon   ring   tornado

1. Substance

1. _____

2. Having to do with the study of the universe

2. _____

3. Band of particles that orbits a planet

3. _____

4. Representation; picture

4. _____

5. Gaseous mass surrounding a planet or star

5. _____

6. Natural satellite of a planet

6. _____

7. Examine carefully

7. _____

8. Violently whirling column of air

8. _____

9. Round; moving in a spiral

9. _____

10. Distance from bottom to top

10. _____

11. The concealing of one celestial body by another

11. _____

12. Flat and even

12. _____

13. Form of radiant energy that enables us to see

13. _____

__ __ __ __ __   __ __ __ __ __ __ __ __
1 2 3 4 5   6 7 8 9 10 11 12 13

What Makes Nerves Grow?

How does a single fertilized egg perform the incredible feat of turning into a complex organism with many different kinds of cells that number in the millions? The process is still not fully understood. But in the 1940s, a female Italian biologist experimenting with chick embryos in Turin, Italy, added an important piece to the puzzle. She found that when budding limbs were removed, nerve cells that had begun to travel from the developing nervous system toward these limbs died. However, when new limbs were grafted onto the embryo, the nerve cells started to grow again. She concluded that the limbs released a substance that caused nerve cells to grow.

In the 1950s this same biologist continued her work at Washington University in St. Louis, Missouri. She transplanted cells from cancerous tumors into three-day-old chick embryos. Within days, nerve fibers grew out from nearby clusters of nerve cells and surrounded the cancer cells. She concluded that the tumors, like the budding limbs, released a material that quickened the growth of nerve cells. With biochemist Stanley Cohen, she isolated and identified the mysterious substance called NGF (Nerve Growth Factor) released by tumors. For that discovery, they shared the 1986 Nobel Prize for Physiology or Medicine.

To find the name of this female recipient of the 1986 Nobel Prize, circle the one word that doesn't belong in each row of words. Then, starting with row 1, write the last letter of each circled word.

Puzzle 13   What Makes Nerves Grow?

1. animal	creature	organism	factor
2. separate	semi	extract	remove
3. growth	experiment	tumor	cancer
4. media	graft	attach	join
5. cell	bud	grow	develop
6. medicine	limb	branch	extension
7. biol	chem	phys	rev
8. name	identify	multi	recognize
9. discharge	emit	organism	release
10. disperse	spread	strew	embryo
11. prize	million	award	tribute
12. mass	cluster	group	transplant
13. extra	discover	find	unearth
14. travel	fiber	thread	string
15. embryo	fetus	unborn	basic
16. nerve	skin	muscle	mini
17. matter	brighten	substance	material
18. encompass	anti	surround	enclose

__ __ __ __   __ __ __ __ - __ __ __ __ __ __ __ __ __ __
1   2   3   4   5   6   7   8   9 10 11 12 13 14 15 16 17 18

The Big Brown Paper Bag

Every day thousands of brown paper bags are carried home from supermarkets and other stores all over the country. Yet few consumers realize that the machine that cuts, folds, and pastes the square or rectangular bottoms of these bags was invented in the late 1860s by an American woman.

This unusual inventor had little formal education. She built the machine while she was employed in a paper bag company in Massachusetts. There she had observed workers performing the time-consuming task of cutting, folding, and pasting bag bottoms by hand. Later in life, this mechanically oriented woman patented other machines, including a rotary engine and a machine for cutting shoe soles.

The name of this female inventor appears in code on the next page. In this code, each number stands for a different letter of the alphabet, as noted. Write the appropriate letter above each of the numbered spaces.

Name _____ Date _____

Puzzle 14   The Big Brown Paper Bag

<u> </u> <u> </u> <u> </u> <u> </u> <u> </u> <u> </u> <u> </u> <u> </u>   <u> </u> <u> </u> <u> </u> <u> </u> <u> </u> <u> </u>

13 1 18 7 1 18 5 20   11 14 9 7 8 20

A = 1	N = 14
B = 2	O = 15
C = 3	P = 16
D = 4	Q = 17
E = 5	R = 18
F = 6	S = 19
G = 7	T = 20
H = 8	U = 21
I = 9	V = 22
J = 10	W = 23
K = 11	X = 24
L = 12	Y = 25
M = 13	Z = 26

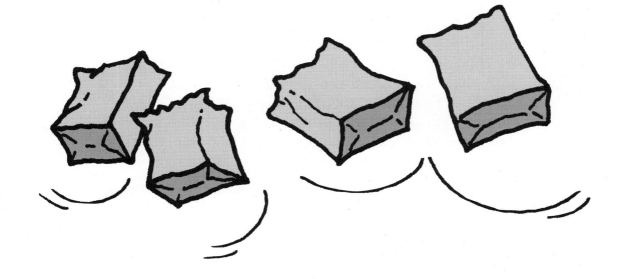

Fermat's Last Theorem: A Partial Solution

The Pythagorean theorem devised in ancient Greece concerns right triangles. A right triangle is a triangle that has an angle that contains 90 degrees and looks like the corner of a square. The side of the triangle opposite the right angle is called the hypotenuse. The Pythagorean theorem states that in a right triangle, the sum of each of the other two sides multiplied by itself equals the hypotenuse multiplied by itself.

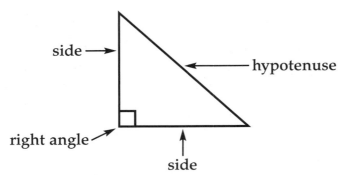

Pierre de Fermat was a seventeenth-century lawyer who studied mathematics as a hobby. In a page margin of one of his math textbooks, he wrote a note where the Pythagorean theorem was being discussed. Basically, his note stated that the sum of two numbers, each multiplied by itself more than twice, cannot equal a third number multiplied by itself more than twice when all numbers are multiplied by themselves the same number of times. No proof of this statement was ever found, and the note became known as Fermat's Last Theorem.

However, in 1994, Andrew Wiles, an English mathematician working at Princeton University, published a proof. News stories about his achievement referred to other mathematicians whose prior work had contributed to his success. But nowhere was credit given to a late eighteenth- and early nineteenth-century female French theoretical mathematician who had proved the correctness of Fermat's Last Theorem in special cases involving prime numbers. Prime numbers have no common whole number divisor except the number 1. Her work was a major step toward proving Fermat's Last Theorem.

The word search on the next page contains clues that lead to the name of this French woman mathematician. The 20 words in the list are hidden in the puzzle. The words can be read horizontally, vertically, or diagonally. Locate and circle each word. A letter may appear in more than one word, so some of the circles may overlap. After you have circled all the words on the list, solve the puzzle at the bottom of the page.

Name _____ Date _____

Puzzle 15   Fermat's Last Theorem: A Partial Solution

degrees	devise	divisor	equation	geometry	Greece	hypotenuse
last	limited	multiply	number	origin	prime	proof
side	solution	square	sum	theorem	triangle	

1. L B S Q U A R E K O H S
2. I M U L T I P L Y Z Y O
3. M E Q U A T I O N T P L
4. I N U M B E R G H D O U
5. T R I A N G L E M R T T
6. E Z W V C B O C Y K E I
7. D L D E G R E E S P N O
8. G E O M E T R Y P S U N
9. R P R M R M P R U J S Y
10. E R I S F C O M D P E L
11. E I G U I O L A S T E O
12. C M I V F D I V I S O R
13. E E N C M D E V I S E Z

Now Write

The 2nd circled letter in line 1   ___
The 11th circled letter in line 2   ___
The 11th circled letter in line 3   ___
The 8th circled letter in line 4   ___
The 3rd circled letter in line 5   ___
The 1st circled letter in line 6   ___

The 4th circled letter in line 7   ___
The 2nd circled letter in line 8   ___
The 1st circled letter in line 9   ___
The 6th circled letter in line 10 ___
The 7th circled letter in line 11 ___
The 3rd circled letter in line 12 ___
The 3rd circled letter in line 13 ___

Battling AIDS: The Creation of AZT

The mere mention of AIDS (Acquired Immune Deficiency Syndrome) frightens many persons. The virus that causes AIDS destroys white blood cells called T lymphocytes, which help cells fight infections in the body. Eventually so few T lymphocytes remain that many persons with AIDS become very sick and die from diseases that rarely kill healthy individuals.

What can be done to help people suffering from AIDS? In 1988 five people working for a U. S. pharmaceutical company, co-patented a drug called AZT (azidothymidine). Two of these co-inventors were women. One was the chemistry group leader in the company's laboratories and the other was the company's retro-virus specialist. Although AZT does not cure AIDS, it does slow the reproduction of the AIDS virus.

Since 1988, new drugs that fight AIDS have been developed, tested, and found to help AIDS sufferers. These drugs include protease inhibitors, which interrupt the reproduction of the AIDS virus and are often very effective. However, for many HIV-infected individuals, AZT remains an important part of their treatment.

Find the names of the two female co-discoverers of AZT by solving the two puzzles on the next page. The first puzzle tells you the chemist and the second the virus specialist. Circle one letter in each box from left to right to make three 4-letter words in Puzzle A and two 4-letter and one 5-letter word in Puzzle B. Use the clues to help find the words. All words appear in the text above. After you have circled the correct letters, start at the top and write the remaining letters from left to right at the bottom of the page.

Name _____ Date _____

Puzzle 16   Battling AIDS: The Creation of AZT

Puzzle A

1.	TJ	EA	SN	ET
2.	TC	UR	IR	ED
3.	SE	OI	CU	TK

1. Trial to prove a drug's value
2. Restore to health; rid of a harmful condition
3. Ill

— — — — —   — — — — — —

Puzzle B

1.	MA	IA	DR	TS	
2.	DH	AR	SU	TG	
3.	CV	LI	RA	IU	RS

1. Letters that stand for Acquired Immune Deficiency Syndrome
2. Medicine
3. Disease-causing organism

— — — — — —   — — — — — —

An Ichthyosaur Skeleton

In the early 1800s, a passion for collecting fossils led one British female to discover the first complete ichthyosaur skeleton. Ichthyosaurs are extinct marine reptiles that lived between 65 million and 225 million years ago and were native to what is now England. These reptiles had fishlike bodies, four paddle-shaped flippers, and dolphinlike necks and heads.

The woman who discovered this skeleton was an amateur fossil collector. She had no formal training in geology. Geology is the study of the physical characteristics and history of the Earth, including the origin of fossils. However, she had an interest in natural history, read about fossils, and helped her father with his hobby of collecting fossils. One day, while hiking, she noticed bones sticking out from the side of a nearby cliff in the southern English town of Lyme Regis where she lived. She used her personal knowledge to identify the bones as an ichthyosaur skeleton.

Later this fossil collector further examined cliffs in the same area. She discovered the remains of an ancient water reptile called a plesiosaur and the bones of a mature prehistoric flying reptile called a pterodactyl.

To find the name of this woman with a passion, or yen, for learning about fossils, unscramble each jumbled word (on the next page) and write the correct word next to it. Use the clues below the words. All words appear in the text above. After you have unscrambled the words, write the first letter of each word above its number at the bottom of the page.

Puzzle 17 An Ichthyosaur Skeleton

1. RETAUM   __ A __ U R E

2. NATECIN   __ N C I __ __ T

3. LERPITES   __ E __ T __ L E S

4. NEY   __ E __

5. UMARATE   __ M __ T __ U R

6. KENC   __ __ C K

7. VITANE   __ A __ I V E

8. CHAISTHUROY   __ C H __ __ Y __ __ A U R

9. RATLAUN   __ A __ U R __ L

10. GOYGOLE   __ __ O L __ G Y

1. Fully developed
2. Very old
3. Snakes, lizards, turtles, dinosaurs, etc.
4. Strong desire
5. Person who does something without professional training
6. Part of animal joining head to body
7. Belonging to a locality or country; indigenous
8. Extinct marine reptile
9. Produced or existing without human-made changes
10. Study of physical features and history of the Earth

__ __ __ __   __ __ __ __ __ __
1 2 3 4   5 6 7 8 9 10

New Semiconductor Materials

Neutrinos, mesons, and muons are examples of subatomic particles. They are even smaller than the protons and neutrons found in atoms, the tiny units that make up all matter. How do we know about subatomic particles and the forces that bind them in the atom? An African American female theoretical physicist spent the first part of her career devising theories and constructing mathematical models to answer such questions.

A graduate of the Massachusetts Institute of Technology, she was also the first African American woman to receive a Ph.D. from that school. Later she joined AT&T Bell Laboratories, now Lucent Technologies. There her research focused on solid-state physics, the study of atoms so close together that they form solids.

Much of this theoretical physicist's effort was related to semiconductors. These are substances that do not conduct electricity well at low temperatures, but become good conductors when small amounts of certain other substances are added or when heat, light, or electricity is applied. As part of this physicist's work, she developed mathematical models. Laboratory scientists used these models to produce new and improved semiconductors for electronic communications, including telephones, television, and computers.

Later, this female theoretical physicist taught at Rutgers University. In May 1995 she joined the Nuclear Regulatory Commission and assumed the Chair two months later.

To find this theoretical physicist's name, circle the one word that doesn't belong in each row of words on the next page. Then, starting with row 1, write the first letter of each circled word in the spaces at the bottom of the page.

Puzzle 18 New Semiconductor Materials

1.	particle	fragment	speck	semiconductor
2.	hypothesis	question	query	inquiry
3.	bind	improve	fasten	tie
4.	reflect	condense	compress	compact
5.	experiment	laboratory	test	trial
6.	element	loose	free	unattached
7.	force	energy	yesterday	power
8.	gas	liquid	solid	join
9.	conductor	atom	transmitter	conveyer
10.	research	investigation	study	computer
11.	kinetic	neutrino	meson	muon
12.	focus	direct	subatomic	concentrate
13.	observatory	external	outer	exterior
14.	construct	build	neutrino	devise

‾ ‾ ‾ ‾ ‾ ‾ ‾   ‾ ‾ ‾ ‾ ‾ ‾ ‾
1 2 3 4 5 6 7   8 9 10 11 12 13 14

A Hydrometer and an Astrolabe

A mathematician, astronomer, and inventor, this amazing woman became director of the Neoplatonic School at Alexandria in Egypt in approximately A.D. 400. There she lectured on mathematics, astronomy, and the philosophies of Plato and Aristotle.

Personal correspondence between her and one of her student-disciples yields information that she participated in the invention of two important objects. One was a hydrometer, a thin, weighted tube marked with lines and numbers. A hydrometer compares the density of a liquid to the density of water, which is the standard. The other object was an astrolabe, an instrument that measures the angle a heavenly body makes with the horizon. The astrolabe has been replaced by the sextant.

None of this woman's professional writings has been found thus far. However, according to information in texts dating from the Middle Ages, she wrote three books on mathematics. These texts from the Middle Ages also report that she wrote a commentary, or series of notes, explaining a book called the Conics written by a mathematician named Apollonius. The Conics dealt with ideas concerning different-shaped curves that can be obtained by using a flat, level surface called a plane to cut a cone into sections.

To discover the one-word name of this accomplished woman of ancient times, complete the crossword puzzle on the next page. All answers can be found in the text above. After you have completed the puzzle, above each number write the letter in the puzzle square containing the same number.

Puzzle 19   A Hydrometer and an Astrolabe

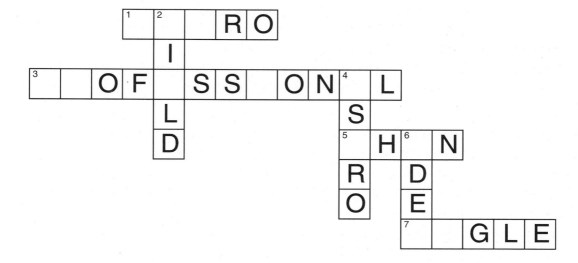

Across
1. Prefix meaning "water"
3. Related to an occupation that is a means of earning a living
5. Narrow; not fat
7. Shape made by two straight lines meeting at a common point

Down
2. Produce (verb); give; surrender
4. Prefix meaning "having to do with stars"
6. Concept; thought

— — — — — — —
1   2   3   4   5   6   7

Breeding Rats: Identical Strains for the Lab

To discover whether new medicines or other treatments are safe and effective for people, scientists often first test their proposed remedies on laboratory animals. Rats are the creatures most frequently selected. Scientists explain that they use rats rather than chipmunks, crabs, or kiwis, for example, because rats produce many generations each year, have large litters, and possess bodies that function in many ways like human bodies.

But rats that are genetically different from one another often react in unlike ways to exactly the same medication or procedure. So in order to be certain that test results reflect nothing but the effects of the treatment, it is essential from the inception of a test to its end that the rats be as genetically identical as possible.

During the first half of the twentieth century, an American female biologist born in New York but working in Pennsylvania carefully bred huge numbers of albino rats through many generations. Her objective was to discover the effects on offspring when closely related rats produce young. However, one result of her work was the development of identical strains of rats that are now crucial to medical laboratories.

Furthermore, when members of an identical strain all possess a specific characteristic, such as an immune system defect or digestive disorder, the effects of new drugs on these particular problems can be studied.

Find this biologist's name by completing the word links on the next page. In these links, the last letter of each word becomes the first letter of the next. Use the clues below the puzzle. All words can be found in the text above. After you have completed the puzzle, write in order the numbered first letter of each word.

Puzzle 20   **Breeding Rats: Identical Strains for the Lab**

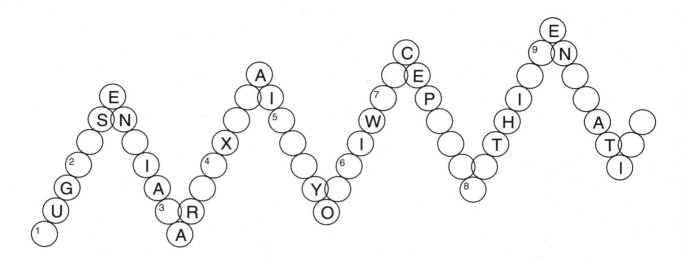

1. Enormous
2. Absolutely necessary
3. Big
4. Make understandable; give the meaning of
5. State on East Coast of the United States (two words)
6. Tailless New Zealand bird with undeveloped wings
7. Beginning
8. Naught; absence of anything
9. Time period between birth of parent and child

‾ ‾ ‾ ‾ ‾   ‾ ‾ ‾ ‾
1 2 3 4 5   6 7 8 9

Crystal Gazing: The Molecular Structure of Vitamin B$_{12}$

Less than one hundred years ago, pernicious anemia was still a deadly blood disease. Anemia is a decrease in the number of red blood cells or the red coloring matter in red blood cells. The word *pernicious* means "very harmful" or "deadly." However, scientists discovered in the 1930s that pernicious anemia can be controlled by eating a diet that includes liver. Then in 1948 crystalline vitamin B$_{12}$, the substance that causes liver's helpful effect, was isolated. Chemists' next objective was to determine the chemical formula of this newly discovered vitamin.

An English female chemist used X-ray crystallography as her approach to finding the formula for vitamin B$_{12}$. A crystal is a solid substance in which the atoms or molecules are arranged in a repeated three-dimensional pattern. In X-ray crystallography, an X-ray beam is directed onto a crystal. Behind the crystal is a photographic plate. When the film is developed, each different kind of crystal reveals its own unique image, which is called a diffraction pattern. The particular pattern is based on the number, kinds, and arrangement of atoms in the crystal.

In the early 1940s, as a young chemist, this woman used X-ray diffraction to determine the chemical structure of penicillin. The penicillin molecule had contained only 39 atoms. Diffraction photos showed that vitamin B$_{12}$ contained more than 1,000 atoms. Nevertheless, she persisted in her search for eight years and was the first person to determine the chemical formula for vitamin B$_{12}$. For this work, she received the 1964 Nobel Prize for Chemistry.

Later advancements in computer technology helped her determine the even more complicated structure of the insulin molecule and produce a graphic representation of it. Insulin is manufactured by the body to help it use sugar.

To find the name of this award-winning chemist with many achievements, complete the crossword tree on the next page. All the words you need are included in the text above.

Puzzle 21 Crystal Gazing: The Molecular Structure of Vitamin B$_{12}$

Across

1. Bending of rays around an obstacle
2. Picture made by a camera (short form)
3. Happening again and again
4. Prefix meaning "crystal"
5. Method of solving practical problems using the findings of science
6. Inquiry to find something
7. Not old
8. Method
9. Aim; purpose; goal
10. Red fluid that circulates through the body
11. Shown by graphs or diagrams
12. Labor; toil
13. Substance produced by the body to help it use sugar
14. An early antibiotic

Down

1. The persistent female British chemist who determined the structure of vitamin B$_{12}$

Crystal Gazing: The Benzene Ring

Another twentieth-century British female chemist also used X-ray crystallography, this time to establish the structure of benzene compounds. These are a special class of organic compounds, compounds that contain carbon. Benzene compounds often have a distinct odor, or aroma.

In 1929 this woman chemist studied crystals of a benzene compound called hexamethyl benzene. Her analysis determined that the benzene ring, a part of all benzene compounds, is a flat, regular six-sided figure called a hexagon. The sides of the hexagon are linked by a carbon atom positioned at each corner.

Later this British female scientist caused diamonds to undergo new X-ray crystallography techniques that she had personally refined. These new techniques enabled her to measure accurately the distance between the carbon atoms in a diamond.

In other projects, she applied X-ray crystallography techniques to medical and biological problems. These included the development of muscle-relaxing drugs and the determination of the nature of kidney stones.

To discover the name of this modern-era woman chemist, write the correct word beside each clue on the next page. All answers appear in the text above. After you have written all the correct words, write the last letter of each word above its number at the bottom of the page.

Puzzle 22   Crystal Gazing: The Benzene Ring

1. Connect; bond   L I __ __

2. Odor; fragrance   A R __ M __

3. Person who observes and experiments in order to
   determine the nature of what is being investigated   S C I __ __ __ I S __

4. Determine; prove   E S __ A B __ I __ __

5. Solid substance in which atoms or molecules are
   arranged in a repeated three-dimensional pattern   C R __ S T __ __

6. Class of compounds containing a ring of six
   carbon atoms   B E __ Z E __ __ __

7. Determine the dimensions of an object   M E __ __ U R __

8. Element in all organic compounds   C A __ B __ __

9. Connected with the science that deals with animal and
   plant life   B I __ __ O G __ C A __

10. Experience; endure   U N D __ __ G __

11. Six-sided figure   H E X __ __ __ __ __

12. Detailed examination to determine nature and
    relationship of parts   A N __ __ Y S I __

13. Gem made of nearly pure carbon   D I __ M O __ __

14. A memorable period of time   E __ __

15. Connected with the practice or study of medicine   M E __ __ C A __

16. Purify; make more precise   R __ F I __ __

___ ___ ___ ___ ___ ___ ___ ___   ___ ___ ___ ___ ___ ___ ___ ___
 1   2   3   4   5   6   7   8   9 10 11 12 13 14 15 16

A People-Safe Fungus Killer

The practice of medicine changed forever in the 1940s. During that decade, powerful new antibiotics such as penicillin and streptomycin were introduced. Unfortunately, these new drugs that killed many disease-causing organisms in people also caused the destruction of certain bacteria that controlled the growth of funguses in the human body. A new, potent fungicide safe for human beings was urgently needed.

Two New York women scientists, a chemist and a microbiologist, working in state public health laboratories, were the first to develop such a substance. After evaluating and culturing numerous soil samples, these two scientists isolated a yellow powder that they named nystatin. The commercial form of nystatin appeared in 1954 as Mycostatin.

This drug proved even more successful than anticipated. Besides curing human fungal infections, nystatin slowed the spoilage of fruits and livestock feed and even prevented mold from growing on paintings and manuscripts damaged by water.

The names of the discoverers of this first fungicide safe for human beings can be found by solving the puzzles on the next page. The first puzzle names the chemist and the second the microbiologist. Circle one letter in each box from left to right to make one 3-letter word and two 4-letter words in Puzzle A and one 4-letter and two 5-letter words in Puzzle B. Use the clues below each puzzle. All words appear in the text above. After you have circled the correct letters, start at the top and write the remaining letters from left to right in the spaces at the bottom of the page.

Puzzle 23   A People-Safe Fungus Killer

Puzzle A

1.	NR	EA	CW
2.	HS	OE	IL	BL
3.	FR	EO	EW	ND

1. Never existing before
2. Surface layer of Earth
3. Food given to animals; fodder

— — — — — — — —   — — — — — — —

Puzzle B

1.	EM	OL	IL	DZ
2.	CA	BA	UE	TS	HE
3.	HS	PA	ZO	EI	NL

1. Kind of growth caused by fungi, in presence of dampness
2. That which produces a result
3. Damage (verb); decay (verb)

— — — — — — — —   — — — — — — —

The Nuclear Shell

Physicists have known for many years that electrons move at different energy levels around the nucleus of an atom. These energy levels are often referred to as orbits, or shells. But in the early 1950s, a German-born American female physicist working at The University of Chicago startled the scientific world by proposing that the protons and neutrons inside the nucleus likewise existed in definite energy levels or shells.

Each shell, she stated, could hold only a specific number of protons and neutrons. On the basis of her shell model of the nucleus, she predicted accurately that the most stable nuclei are those where the number of protons or neutrons result in filled shells. For this theoretical work, she shared the 1963 Nobel Prize for Physics with J. Hans D. Jensen, who had independently developed a nuclear shell theory.

To find the 1963 female recipient of the Nobel Prize for Physics, circle the one word that doesn't belong in each row of words on the next page. Then, starting with row 1, write the last letter of each circled word above its number at the bottom of the page.

Puzzle 24   **The Nuclear Shell**

1.	shell	orbit	path	helium
2.	atom	inertia	molecule	compound
3.	theory	number	hypothesis	proposition
4.	amount	total	sum	nuclei
5.	alpha	completed	filled	occupied
6.	model	sum	example	plan
7.	predict	foretell	plasma	prophesy
8.	inert	stable	energy	fixed
9.	common	shared	freeze	joint
10.	neutron	electron	proton	nuclear

__ __ __ __ __   __ __ __ __ __
1 2 3 4 5   6 7 8 9 10

Individual Room Temperature Controls

Thermostats in individual hotel rooms and offices are now a common sight. These thermostats allow occupants to control the temperature of the room or sometimes a group of rooms that are close together. However, in 1919, when an African American female inventor received a patent for a special kind of gas home-heating furnace, the idea of individually regulating room temperatures was new.

The heating furnace designed by this woman inventor included heating units arranged so that they branched out from a central furnace. Each heating unit was equipped with independent temperature controls. Hot-air ducts extended from these heating units to different rooms in the house.

As a result of this furnace's unique construction, the air in separate rooms could be heated to different temperatures depending upon the desires and needs of the occupants. When rooms were empty, the heating unit or units leading to those rooms could be set so that no heated air was released to them. This prevented the waste of energy and resulted in lower heating costs.

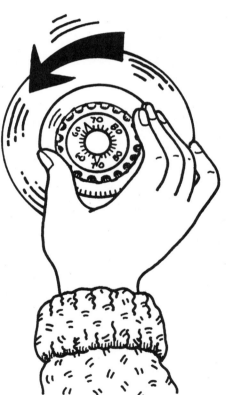

To find the name of this woman inventor of a furnace that allowed individual room temperature controls, on the next page write the correct word next to its definition. All words can be found in the word box and in the text above. After you have written all the correct words, write the first letter of each word above its number at the bottom of the page.

Puzzle 25   Individual Room Temperature Controls

air	arrange	central	equip	extend	individual
kind	lower	patent	regulate	release	

1. Put in correct or suitable order

1. _____

2. Reduced in amount

2. _____

3. Existing as a separate thing

3. _____

4. Main; middle

4. _____

5. Provide with what is needed; furnish

5. _____

6. Document granting the sole right to make, sell, or gain profit from an invention for a certain number of years

6. _____

7. Invisible mixture of gases that surrounds the earth

7. _____

8. Control; adjust to a particular degree

8. _____

9. Sort (noun); type (noun)

9. _____

10. Stretch out for a certain distance

10. _____

11. Let go; set free

11. _____

__ __ __ __ __   __ __ __ __ __ __
1 2 3 4 5   6 7 8 9 10 11

Nuclear Fission

Have you ever wondered who created expressions such as "greenhouse effect," "genetic engineering," "big bang," "Milky Way," and "nuclear fission"? Often, the originators cannot be identified. But in the case of nuclear fission, the term was first used by a woman physicist born in Austria in 1878.

In the 1930s, along with Otto Hahn and Fritz Strassman, she conducted research on neutron-bombarded uranium. In 1938 she was forced to flee Nazi Germany and moved to Sweden.

Hahn and Strassman continued their work and demonstrated that barium is produced when a uranium nucleus is hit by neutrons. From Sweden, this woman physicist, along with her nephew, Otto Frisch, suggested that the neutrons had caused the uranium nucleus to split, leaving two smaller nuclei in place of one large nucleus. She borrowed the word *fission* from biology to describe the process. In biology, fission is a process that often occurs in simple plants and animals. The parent divides into two or more approximately equal parts and each part becomes an independent individual. In 1966, jointly with Otto Hahn and Fritz Strassman, she received the Enrico Fermi Award for achievements in atomic energy.

The word search on the next page contains clues that lead to the name of this early investigator of nuclear fission. Find the 19 words. The words can be read horizontally, vertically, or diagonally. Locate each word and circle it. A letter may appear in more than one word, so some of the circles may overlap. After you have circled all the words on the list, follow the instructions underneath.

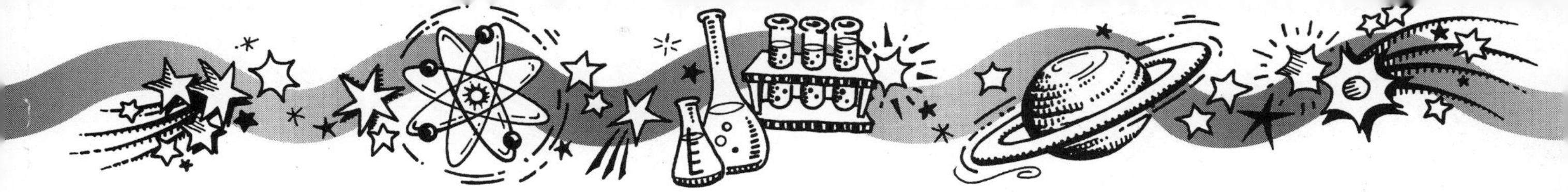

Name ______________________________ Date ____________

Puzzle 26 Nuclear Fission

atomic	beta	bomb	cube	elements	energy	Fermi
fission	gamma	neutrons	nuclear	ore	proton	ray
reactor	stable	tag	theory	uranium		

1.	F	N	E	L	E	M	E	N	T	S	B
2.	I	E	G	A	M	M	A	G	T	E	C
3.	S	U	U	T	X	O	R	A	T	O	R
4.	S	T	R	O	R	G	B	A	R	E	Z
5.	I	R	A	M	D	L	Z	R	A	N	N
6.	O	O	N	I	E	O	E	C	Y	E	U
7.	N	N	I	C	R	D	T	C	U	R	C
8.	N	S	U	E	C	O	R	T	A	G	L
9.	X	B	M	P	R	O	T	O	N	Y	E
10.	E	Y	T	H	E	O	R	Y	X	N	A
11.	B	O	M	B	Z	F	E	R	M	I	R

Now write:

The 4th circled letter in line 1 ___
The 1st circled letter in line 2 ___
The 1st circled letter in line 3 ___
The 8th circled letter in line 4 ___

The 4th circled letter in line 5 ___
The 5th circled letter in line 6 ___
The 3rd circled letter in line 7 ___
The 5th circled letter in line 8 ___
The 8th circled letter in line 9 ___
The 4th circled letter in line 10 ___
The 7th circled letter in line 11 ___

An Absence of Symmetry

Every day we see numerous symmetrical objects—objects identical or very similar in form on both sides of a real or imaginary dividing line. For example, the left and right sides of the human face are symmetrical, as are the two halves of a leaf.

But in physics, symmetry means that the laws of physics remain unchanged in a mirror image system. A system is an arrangement of related things to form a whole, such as the solar system. A mirror image is a view with the right side seen as though it were the left and vice versa. The importance of symmetry in physics is that much of the behavior of a system can be predicted if symmetry can be assumed.

Prior to 1956, all processes ever discovered in physics had been spatially symmetric. But in that year, an American female physicist, who had been born in China, studied beta particles—electrons with a positive charge given off by the nucleus during radioactive decay of a form of the element cobalt. She observed that these beta particles exhibited a preferred direction of emission that depended on the direction of spin of the emitting nucleus. The emission process would not be identical in a mirror image system and the laws of physics would not remain unchanged.

This discovery had been predicted by two Nobel-Prize-winning physical theorists. However, this woman physicist's experimental work helped confirm their hypothesis and called into question some fundamental assumptions of physics based on the behavior of matter the size of an atom or larger. Today, scientists are still searching for a general unifying theory that will explain why certain behavior of atomic and subatomic particles is different.

Solve the puzzle on the next page to find the name of this female physicist. First unscramble each jumbled word and write the correct word next to it. Use the clues below the words. All correctly written words appear in the text above. After you have unscrambled the words, write the first letter of each word above its number at the bottom of the page.

Puzzle 27 An Absence of Symmetry

1. TALCBO   __ O B __ __ T

2. TOPSHEISHY   __ Y __ __ T H __ S I S

3. CLADENITI   __ D E N __ __ __ A L

4. BIXIETH   __ X __ I B __ __ __

5. SLENUCU   __ U __ __ E U S

6. MYSTRYME   __ Y M __ __ __ R Y

7. FLAH   __ __ L F

8. GRAINYAIM   __ M A G __ __ __ R Y

9. GUCHNANDE   __ N C H __ __ G __ __

10. BLEON   __ O __ E L

11. REGALEN   __ E N __ __ A L

12. HELOW   __ __ O L __

13. FUNYI   __ __ I F Y

1. Element whose emission of beta particles helped show an exception to the laws of symmetry
2. Possible explanation of a set of observations or experimental results
3. Exactly the same
4. Expose to view; display
5. Central part of an atom
6. Similarity of form on either side of a dividing line; laws of physics remain unchanged in a mirror image system
7. Either of two equal parts of a thing
8. Existing only in the mind; unreal
9. Remaining the same
10. Swedish inventor of dynamite who established international prizes
11. Applying to the whole class; common
12. Entirety; unity
13. Combine into one

__ __ __ __ __ - __ __ __ __ __ __   __ __
1 2 3 4 5   6 7 8 9 10 11   12 13

The First Computer Compiler

Frequently we hear about new, high-powered computers with ever larger random-access memory, or RAM for short. But as we tap away at computer keyboards, we rarely think about the complex interiors of computers that enable them to operate smoothly and reach accurate, nongarbled solutions to our problems.

For example, in 1952, an American woman mathematician, who had already been a career naval officer, developed the first compiler, a special kind of computer program, while she was working at what was then Remington-Rand Corporation. Before the invention of this compiler, computer programmers wrote long instructions in binary code for each new piece of software. Binary code consists solely of 0s and 1s. It is called "computer language" because computers understand information only if it is presented in binary code.

The use of binary code to create new software is time-consuming and can result in many errors. This woman mathematician wrote a new program that gave "call numbers" to groups of binary instructions common to almost all programs. The binary instructions were stored in the computer's memory. Each time the computer needed to use these common instructions, the compiler had the computer refer to the call numbers. In this way the computer found the appropriate computer language without programmers having to write out the instructions in binary code.

A later version of this compiler was widely used, preparing the way for the development of programming languages. These are symbols, letters, and numbers that represent frequently used groups of computer- or machine-language instructions.

This same female mathematician also introduced the idea that computer programs could be written in English or in any other spoken language. In her opinion, each letter of the alphabet was just a type of symbol that the computer could learn to recognize and convert into machine code. To accomplish this task, she developed a compiler known as FLOW-MATIC. In the early 1960s, much of FLOW-MATIC was used in the design of COBOL, a universal computer language.

To discover the name of this creative female mathematician, complete the crossword puzzle on the next page. All answers can be found in the text above. After you have completed the puzzle, write above each number the letter in the puzzle square containing the same number.

Puzzle 28 The First Computer Compiler

Across
1. Confuse; mix up
3. Free from errors
5. Every single one
7. Function (verb); work (verb)
9. Force or energy that is put to work
10. Mistake

Down
2. Attain; achieve
4. Program that enables computer to find in its memory and use binary instructions common to many programs
6. Receive through the ear; be informed of
8. Code of instructions telling a computer which operations to perform
11. Abbreviation for random-access memory

___ ___ ___ ___ ___   ___ ___ ___ ___ ___ ___
 1   2   3   4   5   6   7   8   9   10 11

Stars That Brighten and Dim

Twinkle, twinkle little star . . . . All stars twinkle as changes in the Earth's atmosphere alter the bending of starlight. But when we gaze at the night sky, we seldom realize that some stars do more than just twinkle. Some stars repeatedly brighten and dim at regular intervals. Astronomers call these stars Cepheids because the first such star discovered was named delta Cephei in the constellation Cepheus. The time between consecutive bright or dull phases is called a pulsation.

In 1912 a female American astronomer working at the Harvard Observatory used photographic methods to discover that the brighter the Cepheid, the longer the time between pulsations. More precisely, she discovered that the time between pulsations of Cepheids is proportional to their average brightness. Subsequent astronomers used this relationship to help them calculate the distances from Earth to Cepheids and to the galaxies in which they exist.

Find the name of this notable woman astronomer by solving the puzzle on the next page. First, circle one letter in each box from left to right to make one 5-letter word, one 7-letter word, and one 4-letter word. Use the clues below the puzzle to help find the words. All words appear in the text above. After you have circled the correct letters, start at the top and write the remaining letters from left to right in the spaces at the bottom of the page.

Puzzle 29   **Stars That Brighten and Dim**

1.	PH	EH	AN	SR	IE	
2.	EC	TE	TP	HA	EL	EI	DA
3.	VS	IT	AT	RT		

1. Repeating stage of change in brightness
2. Class of star that repeatedly brightens and dims
3. Luminous object seen as a point of light in the sky

— — — — — — — — — — — — — — — — — —

Computer Systems for NASA

As part of its space exploration and information-gathering activities, the National Aeronautics and Space Administration (NASA) uses computer systems. A female African American data analyst and mathematician was an important contributor to the design and development of several of these systems.

Her career at NASA extended from 1964 to 1995. During that time, she developed computer systems that enabled computers to collect data, automatically compute with it, and use the results to operate space satellite control centers. She also participated in the development of image-processing data systems for three Landsat satellites. These satellites orbited high above the Earth and took aerial photographs. The satellites transmitted back data about the Earth's surface features and resources. One use of this information was to preserve our natural environment.

Later, this woman computer data analyst and mathematician helped develop SPAN, a computer network of about 2,700 computers worldwide. SPAN is now an important part of the Internet.

But these weren't this talented woman's only accomplishments. In 1980 she patented a device that transmitted visual illusions. Her invention used concave mirrors at both the transmitting and receiving ends. These mirrors created three-dimensional images in the space in front of the receiving screen. The human eye viewed these images as real, although they were optical illusions.

To find the name of this data analyst, mathematician, and inventor, write the correct word next to each clue on the next page. All answers appear in the text above. After you have written all the correct words, write the first letter of each word above its number at the bottom of the page.

Puzzle 30   Computer Systems for NASA

1. Connected with or based on seeing   __ I S __ A L

2. By means of aircraft or flying   __ E R __ A L

3. U.S. satellite for gathering and transmitting data
   about the Earth's surface and resources   __ A N __ S A __

4. Living and nonliving factors that make up
   surroundings   __ __ V I R __ __ __ E N T

5. Something that is available for use   __ __ S O __ R C E

6. An unreal interpretation of what one sees   __ L __ U S __ O N

7. Organ of sight   __ Y __

8. Send from one place to another   __ __ A N S __ I T

9. Situated far above the ground   __ __ G H

10. Related to the sense of sight   __ __ T I __ A L

11. Smooth surface that reflects the images of objects   __ I R __ O R

12. Regulating itself   __ __ T O __ A __ I C

13. Object made by people and rocketed into orbit
    around the Earth, moon, etc.   __ A T __ __ __ I T E

__ __ __ __ __ __ __   __ __ __ __ __ __
1 2 3 4 5 6 7   8 9 10 11 12 13

Air and Noise Pollution Controls

During the nineteenth century, as machine-made goods poured out of factories and smoke poured out of factory chimneys, polluted air hung heavily over American industrial cities. In 1879 a woman inventor living in New York City tackled this problem. She patented a procedure designed to direct emissions from factory smokestacks into water tanks. The dirty water would then be flushed into city sewers and the outflow disposed of via underground drains along with other waste water.

In 1891 this female inventor also obtained a patent on a device aimed at muting the roar of electric railways racing on elevated tracks through New York City. Her device used a wooden boxlike frame. She painted the box with tar, lined the box with cotton, and filled it with sand. This apparatus was attached to the underside of the elevated railways. The device absorbed the rail vibrations causing the loud sounds.

After she received her patent, she sold her rights to New York City's Metropolitan Railroad. Several other inventors, including Thomas Edison, had worked on this problem previously, without success.

To find the name of this female inventor who worked to relieve two environmental pollution phenomena, complete the crossword tree on the next page. Use the clues below the puzzle. All the words are included in the text above.

Copyright © 1999 Good Year Books.

Name _____ Date _____

Puzzle 31   Air and Noise Pollution Controls

```
                              1 A C H │   N E
       2 P H │   O M │ N │      A I L │   │ Y
           4 F │ C │   O R │   3
                              5 A   T │ R
               6 V │            
                              7     U D
           8 D I │   C │       
                              9     U T │   O W
       10 E M I │   │   │
```

Across

1. Device for doing work
2. Experiences apparent to the senses and that can be scientifically described
3. Track with parallel steel rails for guiding wheels
4. Manufacturing plant
5. Colorless transparent liquid in Earth's rivers, lakes, and oceans
6. By way of; by means of
7. Noisy; making sounds of great intensity
8. Guide (verb); lead (verb)
9. Material that leaves as a liquid or gas
10. Discharge (noun)

Down

1. Inventor of air and noise pollution controls

Conservation of Energy: Early Statements

The principle of conservation of energy states that within a system, energy can be neither created nor destroyed but can only change in form. No one knows who first proposed this scientific law. However, as early as 1834, a Scottish woman who wrote about science and mathematics had stated that a unity of different kinds of energy exists.

These words are obscure, and during her life she never stated an actual general principle of conservation of energy. But her book *On the Connexions of the Physical Sciences* interprets her thoughts and yields more than just oblique or indirect references to such a principle.

She wrote that the progress of modern science simplifies the laws of nature and unites them through general principles. As examples, she stated that eventually light and heat will be referred to as the same agent and that the mechanisms or processes that convert and relate magnetism, electricity, and chemistry are the new connection. Experiments later verified many of her ideas.

To find the author of these forerunners to the principle of conservation of energy, unscramble each jumbled word (on the next page) and write the correct word next to it. Use the clues below the words. All correctly written words appear in the text above. After you have unscrambled the words, write the first letter of each word above its number at the bottom of the page.

Name _____   Date _____

Puzzle 32   Conservation of Energy: Early Statements

1. SMICHNAME   _ _ C H _ _ I S M

2. NAGET   _ G _ N T

3. TALEER   _ E _ A T E

4. LIDEY   _ _ E L D

5. FLIPMISY   _ I M _ _ _ F Y

6. QUIBOLE   _ B L _ Q U E

7. MISTANGEM   _ A G _ _ _ _ S M

8. PAXLEEM   _ X _ M _ L E

9. FREER   _ E _ E R

10. FEVIRY   _ E R _ F Y

11. PERTRETIN   _ _ T E R _ _ E T

12. FILE   _ _ F E

13. WAL   _ A W

14. TELERICTYIC   _ _ E C _ _ I C _ TY

1. Means or process for doing something
2. Active force or substance producing an effect
3. Connect; show a connection between
4. Furnish; produce
5. Make less complicated
6. Slanted; indirect
7. Attractive force acting between materials such as iron that can attract like materials
8. Typical instance
9. Direct attention to; allude
10. Prove to be true
11. Explain; make understandable
12. Time a person is alive
13. Scientific principle
14. Electric current

_ _ _ _   _ _ _ _ _ _ _ _ _ _
1 2 3 4   5 6 7 8 9 10 11 12 13 14

Adding to the Periodic Table

During the 1920s, chemists worked feverishly to discover new elements and complete the Periodic Table. This table was an attempt to arrange and organize all the elements on Earth according to atomic number, the number of protons in the nucleus.

In 1925 a female German chemist working with her husband in Berlin contributed to the Periodic Table by discovering rhenium, element number 75. The rhenium they discovered was in columbite, a rare mineral composed mainly of the elements iron and niobium.

Rhenium is a dense, rare, silvery white metal with a high melting point. This element is used in alloys that must withstand great temperatures. Alloys are a mixture of metals, usually formed by melting them together.

This same woman chemist suggested to Enrico Fermi in 1934 that when he had bombarded uranium atoms with slow-moving neutrons, the uranium nuclei had split into two approximately equal fragments. Fermi, however, remained unconvinced because his results had been unclear. But in 1939, when Otto Frisch, a male physicist, made the same suggestion, Fermi accepted the idea. He went on to build the first nuclear reactor.

Find the name of this significant woman chemist by first completing the word search on the next page. The sixteen words in the list are hidden horizontally, vertically, or diagonally. Locate each word and circle it. A letter may appear in more than one word, so some of the circles may overlap. After you have circled all the words, follow the instructions under the list.

Puzzle 33   Adding to the Periodic Table

add	alloy	dense	discover	earth	equal
fragment	melt	mineral	mixture	periodic	rare
rhenium	table	trace	work		

1.   R   M   I   N   E   R   A   L   P   F
2.   H   I   D   I   S   C   O   V   E   R
3.   E   X   E   A   R   T   H   G   R   A
4.   N   T   A   B   L   E   B   M   I   G
5.   I   U   A   R   Z   Q   V   J   O   M
6.   U   R   D   M   T   U   N   A   D   E
7.   M   E   D   R   E   A   L   E   I   N
8.   B   R   A   R   E   L   N   Z   C   T
9.   K   C   J   R   O   S   T   Q   U   P
10. E   J   H   Y   E   X   W   O   R   K

Now Write

The 3rd circled letter in line 1   ___
The 3rd circled letter in line 2   ___
The 4th circled letter in line 3   ___

The 1st circled letter in line 4   ___
The 5th circled letter in line 5   ___
The 3rd circled letter in line 6   ___
The 3rd circled letter in line 7   ___
The 2nd circled letter in line 8   ___
The 1st circled letter in line 9   ___
The 7th circled letter in line 10 ___

Avoiding Computer Overload

Have you ever wondered how telephone circuits avoid overloading when large numbers of people make calls at once? The answer lies in computer programs that control the switches on telephone circuits and prevent them from carrying too much power.

The first of these computer programs was developed in the 1950s. At that time the Bell telephone companies were planning to install electronic computers to control telephone switches. These computers were to replace outdated mechanical relay equipment. A relay is a device that senses variations in conditions in an electric circuit and controls electric current accordingly. A circuit is the path over which current flows. The telephone companies needed a way to prevent the new computers from overloading when too many phone calls occurred at the same time.

Through the efforts of a woman with a doctorate in philosophy and a background in mathematics, a solution was achieved. Working in New Jersey at a Bell telephone laboratory, now part of Lucent Technologies, she created and patented software that measured how busy computers were at different times. Based on this information, the computer regulated the number of calls accepted. She has the honor of receiving one of the first patents for software in the United States. The principles of this switching system are still used today.

To discover the name of this woman inventor, complete the crossword puzzle on the next page. Use the clues. All answers can be found in the text above. After you have completed the puzzle, write above each number under the clues the letter in the puzzle square containing the same number.

Puzzle 34 Avoiding Computer Overload

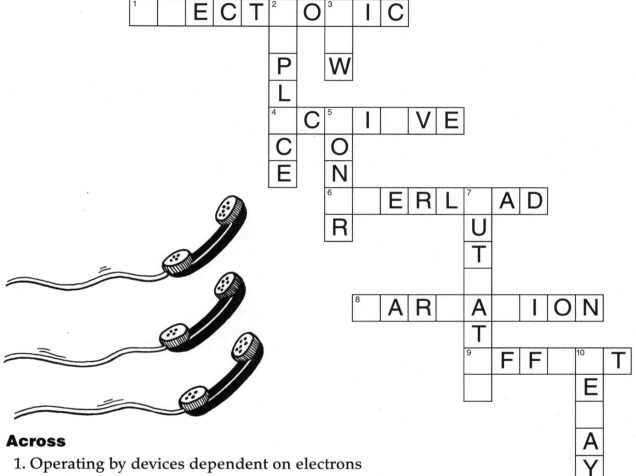

Across

1. Operating by devices dependent on electrons
4. Reach; attain
6. Put too great a burden on
8. Change from a former or usual state
9. Exertion; work

Down

2. Take the position of another person or thing
3. More modern; fresh
5. Credit; renown
7. Behind the times
10. Device that controls electric current in a circuit

‾1‾ ‾2‾ ‾3‾ ‾4‾   ‾5‾ ‾6‾ ‾7‾ ‾8‾ ‾9‾ ‾10‾

The Way Lymph Travels

All cells in the human body are surrounded by a pale yellow fluid called tissue fluid. This fluid consists mainly of water that has moved out of nearby small blood vessels called capillaries. However, tissue fluid also contains certain other substances, including proteins and white blood cells. The proteins nourish the cells and the white blood cells attack disease-causing organisms. Many materials pass between the blood and body cells by traveling through the tissue fluid.

The excess fluid passes through thin-walled vessels called lymph vessels that form a network throughout the body. After tissue fluid is in the lymph vessels, it is called lymph. The largest lymph vessels join veins near the heart and recirculate the lymph.

As late as the beginning of the twentieth century, little specific information was known about how lymph travels in the body. But during the next 25 years, an American female teacher and researcher at Johns Hopkins University carefully investigated lymph vessels and added greatly to our knowledge about them. She concluded that lymph vessels are closed at their connecting ends. Tissue fluids enter by seepage through the vessels' walls and travel in one direction only, back toward the heart. This same researcher also discovered that lymph vessels develop as extensions from veins already in existence and do not form independently.

To find the name of this dedicated woman scientist, write the correct word next to its definition on the next page. All words can be found in the word box and in the text above. After you have written all the correct words, write the first letter of each word above its number at the bottom of the page.

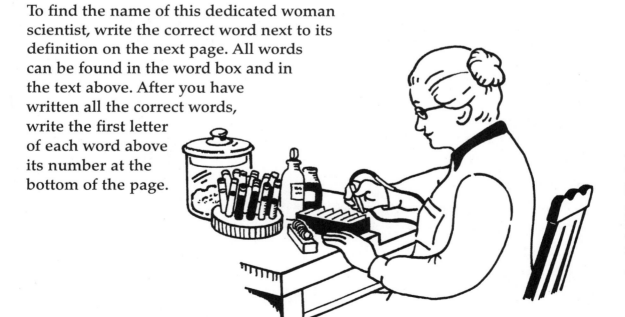

Name _____ Date _____

Puzzle 35 The Way Lymph Travels

attack	body	capillaries	excess	extension
fluid	information	lymph	network	nourish
	organism	researcher	substance	

1. Liquid

1. _____

2. Pale yellow tissue fluid

2. _____

3. Individual plant or animal

3. _____

4. Investigator

4. _____

5. Continuation; addition

5. _____

6. Feed; sustain

6. _____

7. Small blood vessels

7. _____

8. Extra; surplus

8. _____

9. Material; physical matter

9. _____

10. Fight; strike out at

10. _____

11. Entire physical structure and substance

11. _____

12. Knowledge; facts; data

12. _____

13. System of interconnecting parts

13. _____

__ __ __ __ __ __ __ __   __ __ __ __ __
1 2 3 4 5 6 7 8   9 10 11 12 13

Rings That Rotate

Can mathematics really be exciting? A brilliant female theoretical mathematician born in Russia during the second half of the nineteenth century certainly thought so.

Perhaps her enthusiasm began when she was a child and her eccentric uncle read mathematics books to her. Or maybe it started when her parents were short of wallpaper and pasted copies of calculus lectures all over the walls of her room. In any case, much of her life was devoted to mathematical discoveries.

One important contribution was her mathematical proof that Saturn's rings are ovals relative to a single axis, an imaginary line about which the rings are regarded as rotating. She used the theoretical assumption that the rings have a fluid or movable layer. As part of this work, she studied general problems relating to the stability of the motion of ring-shaped liquid bodies.

Later she devised a general mathematical equation for bodies rotating about a fixed point. Earlier mathematicians had considered only cases where a rigid, symmetrical body rotates about a fixed point. This woman mathematician treated more difficult situations where bodies are not symmetrical. For this work, she received the Prix Borodin of the French Academy of Sciences in 1888. The value of the prize was increased from 300 to 500 francs in her case because of the remarkable nature of her work.

Find the name of this amazing woman by solving the puzzle on the next page. Circle one letter in each box from left to right to form three 5-letter words. Use the clues to help find the words. All words appear in the text above. After you have circled the correct letters, start at the top and write the remaining letters from left to right in the spaces under the puzzle.

Puzzle 36   **Rings That Rotate**

1.	PS	OR	ON	YO	FA
2.	KO	OV	AV	AL	SL
3.	EP	OV	IS	NK	YT

1. Establishment of the truth of something
2. Shapes that have the form of eggs
3. A dot; sharp projecting tip

__ __ __ __ __   __ __ __ __ __ __ __ __ __ __
1 2 3 4 5   6 7 8 9 10 11 12 13 14 15

A Boy or a Girl: Chromosomes Determine Sex

What causes some children to be born female and others male? This question has intrigued scientists for years, but it wasn't answered until the early twentieth century.

In 1905 a female biologist working at Bryn Mawr College in Pennsylvania published her findings on the subject. She demonstrated that an offspring's sex is determined by a specific chromosome. Chromosomes are rod-shaped bodies in the cell nucleus.

This biologist had examined mealworms and observed that the female sex cells, or eggs, always contain ten large chromosomes. The male sex cells, or sperm, can contain either ten large chromosomes or nine large ones and a tenth smaller one. The body cells of the mealworm form after the egg and sperm unite. Body cells of the female offspring always include 20 large chromosomes while the body cells of the male offspring always include 19 large chromosomes and one small one. From this evidence, she concluded that sex was determined by the size of a particular chromosome.

The name of this woman who discovered the chromosomal basis of sex can be found by solving the puzzle on the next page. First, circle the one word that doesn't belong in each row of words. Then, starting with row 1, write the first letter of each circled word on the blanks at the bottom of the page.

Name _____ Date _____

Puzzle 37   A Boy or a Girl: Chromosomes Determine Sex

1.	include	nucleus	contain	comprise
2.	rod	stick	egg	shaft
3.	arm	trait	leg	face
4.	offspring	children	twenty	progeny
5.	liver	heart	lung	ingest
6.	split	divide	partition	emerge
7.	examine	inspect	sex	scrutinize
8.	acquire	get	receive	transmit
9.	essential	specific	particular	distinct
10.	rebut	disprove	verify	controvert
11.	latent	hidden	evident	dormant
12.	notice	regular	average	usual
13.	unite	sperm	fuse	combine

__ __ __ __ __ __   __ __ __ __ __ __ __
1 2 3 4 5 6   7 8 9 10 11 12 13

The Electric Arc and Ripple Marks

More than one hundred years ago, a British female physicist-inventor patented a line divider, an instrument that divides a line into any number of equal parts. But this was just the beginning of her illustrious career.

Displaying unusual versatility, she also studied the branch of physics dealing with electricity. In 1902 she published a book containing many formulas relating to the electric arc, the electric current transmitted between the surfaces of two materials that conduct or transmit electricity. The electric path is visible because the air molecules are ionized, which means to gain or lose electrons, and generate light energy during the process.

After her book on the electric arc was finished, this woman physicist and inventor wrote papers about the motions that cause ripple marks in sand. Later her research involved air currents. During World War I, she invented a hand fan that drove off poisonous gas on the battlefield by bringing in fresh air from the area to the rear. This fan was also used to improve ventilation in mine shafts.

To find the name of this versatile physicist-inventor, write the correct word next to each clue on the next page. All answers appear in the text above. After you have written all the correct words, write the last letter of each word above its number at the bottom of the page.

Puzzle 38   The Electric Arc and Ripple Marks

1. Division of a body of learning

   B R _ N C _

2. Outer face of an object

   S U _ F A _ _

3. Instrument for measuring or marking off distances

   D _ V I D _ _

4. Flow of air or water

   C _ _ R E N _

5. Clean; not spoiled or stale

   F R _ S _

6. Part of a surface; region

   A R _ _

7. Set of algebraic symbols expressing a mathematical fact, rule, etc.

   F O R _ _ _ _ _

8. Exhibit (verb); show (verb)

   D I _ P L _ _

9. Place or position at the back

   R E _ _

10. Transmit or carry (electricity)

    C _ _ D U _ _

11. Number between one and three

    T _ _

12. Movement

    M O _ I O _

_ _ _ _ _ _   _ _ _ _ _ _
1 2 3 4 5 6   7 8 9 10 11 12

Radioactive Tracers

Radioactive iodine to diagnose thyroid problems—radioactive phosphorus to locate brain tumors—radioactive nitrogen to reveal lung activity. The use of these medical tools originated barely half a century ago when they filled a yawning gap in medical diagnostic techniques.

During the 1950s, nuclear reactors produced plentiful and relatively inexpensive radioisotopes. These are radioactive forms of elements that in their ordinary form are not radioactive. An American female physicist launched an investigation into the possible medical uses of these isotopes. This search led to her discovery of a technique called radioactive immunoassay (RIA).

RIAs can determine the amount of insulin in a person's blood. Insulin helps the body use sugar and is produced by an organ called the pancreas. A known quantity of insulin is tagged with a radioactive isotope through a chemical reaction. The radioactive insulin is mixed with a known quantity of antibodies against insulin and attaches to these antibodies. An antibody is a protein formed in the body in response to a foreign substance.

If a sample of blood from a person is added to this mixture, the insulin in the blood also attaches to the antibodies and a portion of the radioactive insulin detaches from the antibodies. If the amount of insulin that has been detached is measured, the amount of insulin in the blood sample can be determined exactly.

Today, RIAs help diagnose and analyze a wide range of medical conditions, including drug abuse, viral blood diseases, and pituitary gland problems in young people.

To find the name of the woman physicist who developed RIAs and who, along with Roger Guillemin and Andrew Schally, received the 1977 Nobel Prize for Physiology or Medicine, unscramble each jumbled word (on the next page) and write the correct word next to it. All correctly written words appear in the above text. After you have unscrambled the words, write the first letter of each word above its number under the clues.

Puzzle 39 **Radioactive Tracers**

1. POSTEODAIRIO   __ A __ I O __ __ __ O __ O P E

2. GRANO   __ R __ A N

3. PLAMES   __ A M __ L E

4. BITNADOY   __ __ T I __ O D __

5. HANCLU   __ A U __ C H

6. GINNWAY   __ A W __ __ N G

7. GORENINT   __ I T __ __ G E N

8. GUNOY   __ O __ N G

9. EAZYLAN   __ __ A __ Y Z E

10. TEALCO   __ O __ A T __

11. GRINAITOE   __ R __ G I __ A T E

12. DEWI   __ I D __

1. Radioactive form of an element that isn't ordinarily radioactive
2. Part of an animal or plant composed of specialized tissues
3. Part that is representative of a whole
4. Special protein produced by white blood cells to create immunity
5. Start
6. Wide open; gaping
7. Element whose radioactive isotope is used to reveal lung activity
8. Not old
9. Examine in detail
10. Find
11. Begin; come into existence
12. Broad

__ __ __ __ __ __ __   __ __ __ __ __
1   2   3   4   5   6   7   8   9 10 11 12

An Underwater Telescope

Most history books describe how about 1600 Galileo built one of the earliest telescopes in order to get a better look at the stars and planets. But few history books record that in 1845 an American woman patented an underwater telescope and lamp adapted to locating and examining objects beneath the surface of the sea.

In 1864 in response to naval fighting during the Civil War, this female inventor patented improvements on her telescope. The improvements were designed to help the North destroy Southern underwater warships. These warships were cigar-shaped craft called immersibles and were the forerunners of modern submarines.

Before this woman added the improvements to her underwater telescope, immersibles had posed a special dilemma to the North and a serious threat to human life and property. This was because each immersible was armed with a torpedo intended to sink Northern ships by piercing their hulls. Without her improved underwater telescopes, the crews of Northern ships were unable to detect the immersibles.

To find the name of the little-known woman inventor of an underwater telescope, complete the crossword tree on the next page. Use the clues; all the words you need are included in the text above.

Puzzle 40 An Underwater Telescope

```
              1 U B _ _ _ I N E
      2 S _ _
              3 _ S _ O N _ E
  4 D I _ E M
              5 _ L L
      6 A _
              7 _ A P T
  8 B U I _
              9 _ U M _ N
10 T E _ _ S C _ _
              11 _ E _ O R D
```

Across

1. Warship that operates underwater
2. Ocean
3. Reaction to a stimulus
4. Serious problem; situation in which one must choose between unpleasant alternatives
5. Frame or body of a ship
6. Provide with weapons
7. Adjust to changed or new circumstances
8. Constructed
9. Having qualities typical of people
10. Optical instrument for viewing distant objects
11. Put an account of events in writing

Down

1. Inventor of an underwater telescope

Artificial Radioactive Elements

Imagine creating a new form of an element, a form that had never existed before! A French female chemist did exactly that by bombarding aluminum with alpha particles and producing radioactive phosphorus, an element not ordinarily radioactive. Alpha particles are helium nuclei—helium atoms without their electrons.

In other experiments, she bombarded boron and magnesium with alpha particles and obtained radioactive forms of nitrogen and aluminum, respectively. For producing these new radioactive elements, she and her husband, with whom she had collaborated, received the 1935 Nobel Prize in Chemistry.

But a Nobel Prize was nothing new in this woman's family. Along with Antoine Becquerel, her mother and father had already shared the Nobel Prize in Physics in 1903 for their work on the nature of radioactivity. And in 1911 her mother had again been awarded a Nobel Prize, this time in Chemistry for her discovery of the elements polonium and radium.

To find the name of the woman chemist who in 1935 won a Nobel Prize and in whose family this award seems to run, first complete the word search on the next page. Circle each of the 21 words in the list. The words can be read horizontally, vertically, or diagonally. A letter may appear in more than one word, so some of the circles may overlap. After you have circled all the words, follow the instructions under the puzzle.

Puzzle 41 Artificial Radioactive Elements

alpha	aluminum	artificial	bombard	boron	chemist	create
element	emit	energy	helium	isolate	isotope	judge
magnesium	nitrogen	nuclei	particle	phosphorus	produce	radioactive

1. A L U M I N U M G X Y C
2. R E H B O M B A R D L D
3. T N P E J I S O T O P E
4. I E Z E L E M E N T T R
5. F R R G E I P Y M C G P
6. I G I M K J U D G E I H
7. C Y I S A K Y M Q L S O
8. I T H L O L B W U G O S
9. A O P A R T I C L E L P
10. L H N I T R O G E N A H
11. A Z Y M C H E M I S T O
12. J V B C R E A T E Z E R
13. L D U O X N U C L E I U
14. M F D P R O D U C E O S
15. G R A D I O A C T I V E
16. P T R M A G N E S I U M

Now Write:

The 5th circled letter in line 1 ___
The 1st circled letter in line 2 ___
The 3rd circled letter in line 3 ___
The 8th circled letter in line 4 ___
The 3rd circled letter in line 5 ___

The 4th circled letter in line 6 ___
The 7th circled letter in line 7 ___
The 3rd circled letter in line 8 ___
The 6th circled letter in line 9 ___

The 7th circled letter in line 10 ___
The 8th circled letter in line 11 ___

The 2nd circled letter in line 12 ___
The 3rd circled letter in line 13 ___
The 2nd circled letter in line 14 ___
The 4th circled letter in line 15 ___
The 5th circled letter in line 16 ___

The Human Sugar Cycle

Each time we run, walk, sit, speak, yell, or just sleep, our bodies use energy. Yet, until the 1930s scientists only vaguely understood how this energy is supplied to cells. In that decade, a female biochemist and her husband teaching at Washington University Medical School in St. Louis discovered the basic life processes involved.

These two biochemists determined that whenever we perform even an ordinary activity, sugar stored as glycogen in the liver changes into a simple sugar called glucose. This glucose is transported by the blood to tissues or other organs needing an energy source. There, the cells use the glucose in a process called cellular respiration. A common meaning of respiration is breathing air in and out through the lungs. But in cellular respiration, glucose unites with oxygen to produce carbon dioxide, water, and energy.

However, in situations where muscle cells use glucose but do not have enough oxygen to convert all the glucose to these three products, lactic acid is formed. The blood returns the lactic acid to the liver. The liver either turns the lactic acid into carbon dioxide and water or converts the lactic acid back into glycogen.

While investigating the sugar cycle, this woman biologist and her husband found that each step is helped by a specific protein called an enzyme. They also studied hormones, chemical regulators that affect the sugar cycle. One of these hormones was insulin. This woman biochemist and her husband suggested that insulin may promote reactions in the liver that cause glucose to be stored as glycogen. This theory had a great impact on later investigations into the causes and treatment of diabetes since, in this disease, glucose accumulates in the blood.

For their work on the sugar cycle, this woman chemist and her husband, along with Bernardo Houssay, shared the 1947 Nobel Prize for Medicine or Physiology.

To find the name of the woman chemist, write the correct word next to each clue on the next page. All answers appear in the text above. After you have written all the correct words, write the first letter of each word above its number at the bottom of the page.

Name _____ Date _____

Puzzle 42   The Human Sugar Cycle

1. A simple sugar   _ L U _ _ S E

2. Special proteins that assist reactions
   in the body   _ N Z Y _ _ S

3. Breathing; process of inhaling and
   exhaling air   _ _ S P _ _ A _ I O N

4. Carry from one place to another   _ _ A N S _ _ R T

5. Scream; cry out loudly   _ _ L L

6. Change from one form into another   _ O N V _ _ _ T

7. Usual; common   _ _ D I N _ R Y

8. Activity of substances undergoing a
   chemical change   _ _ A C _ I O N

9. Effect   _ M P _ C T

$\overline{}$ $\overline{}$ $\overline{}$ $\overline{}$ $\overline{}$ $\overline{}$ $\overline{}$ $\overline{}$ $\overline{}$
1 2 3 4 5   6 7 8 9

Women Scientists and Inventors   **85**

ANSWER KEY

Puzzle 1 Gertrude Elion
Puzzle 2 Ada Byron
Puzzle 3 Helen Taussig
Puzzle 4 Emmy Noether
Puzzle 5 Rosalind Franklin
Puzzle 6 Marie Curie
Puzzle 7 Stephanie Kwolek
Puzzle 8 Florence Parpart
Puzzle 9 Margaret Burbidge
Puzzle 10 Barbara Mcclintock
Puzzle 11 Jocelyn Burnell
Puzzle 12 Maria Mitchell
Puzzle 13 Rita Levi-Montalcini
Puzzle 14 Margaret Knight
Puzzle 15 Sophie Germain
Puzzle 16 Janet Rideout and Martha St. Clair
Puzzle 17 Mary Anning
Puzzle 18 Shirley Jackson
Puzzle 19 Hypatia
Puzzle 20 Helen King
Puzzle 21 Dorothy Hodgkin
Puzzle 22 Kathleen Lonsdale
Puzzle 23 Rachel Brown and Elizabeth Hazen
Puzzle 24 Maria Mayer
Puzzle 25 Alice Parker
Puzzle 26 Lise Meitner
Puzzle 27 Chien-Shiung Wu
Puzzle 28 Grace Hopper
Puzzle 29 Henrietta Leavitt
Puzzle 30 Valerie Thomas
Puzzle 31 Mary Walton
Puzzle 32 Mary Somerville
Puzzle 33 Ida Noddack
Puzzle 34 Erna Hoover
Puzzle 35 Florence Sabin
Puzzle 36 Sonya Kovalevsky
Puzzle 37 Nettie Stevens
Puzzle 38 Hertha Ayrton
Puzzle 39 Rosalyn Yalow
Puzzle 40 Sarah Mather
Puzzle 41 Irene Joliot-Curie
Puzzle 42 Gerty Cori

1

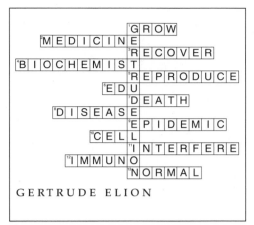

¹GROW
²MEDICINE
³RECOVER
⁴BIOCHEMIST
⁵REPRODUCE
⁶EDU
⁷DEATH
⁸DISEASE
⁹EPIDEMIC
¹⁰CELL
¹¹INTERFERE
¹²IMMUNO
¹³NORMAL

GERTRUDE ELION

2

¹A ²D ³ABS ⁴B RIEF ⁵YEA ⁶R ⁷O ⁸NOTES
(IDEA / DATABS / BRIEFLY / YEAR / DOWN)

ADA BYRON

3

1. Heart
2. Effect
3. Lung
4. Examine
5. Negative
6. Tinge
7. Artery
8. Underneath
9. Structural
10. Surgery
11. Internal
12. Goal

HELEN TAUSSIG

4

1. Einstein
2. Mathematics
3. Matter
4. Yet
5. Number
6. Orderly
7. Energy
8. Theory
9. Hurdle
10. Earth
11. Relativity

EMMY NOETHER

5

1. HR OE SL IA LX
2. IG EN DN FE
3. RX AR AN KY
4. DL IN NA

ROSALIND FRANKLIN

6

1. Magnitude
2. Atomic
3. Radiation
4. Isolate
5. Element
6. Chemistry
7. Uranium
8. Radium
9. Investigate
10. Experiment

MARIE CURIE

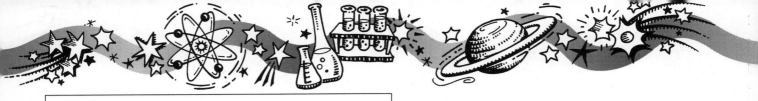

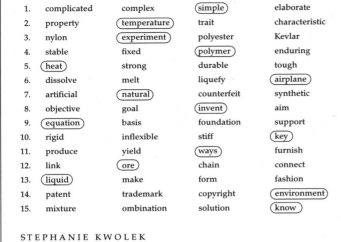

1.	complicated	complex	(simple)	elaborate
2.	property	(temperature)	trait	characteristic
3.	nylon	(experiment)	polyester	Kevlar
4.	stable	fixed	(polymer)	enduring
5.	(heat)	strong	durable	tough
6.	dissolve	melt	liquefy	(airplane)
7.	artificial	(natural)	counterfeit	synthetic
8.	objective	goal	(invent)	aim
9.	(equation)	basis	foundation	support
10.	rigid	inflexible	stiff	(key)
11.	produce	yield	(ways)	furnish
12.	link	(ore)	chain	connect
13.	(liquid)	make	form	fashion
14.	patent	trademark	copyright	(environment)
15.	mixture	ombination	solution	(know)

STEPHANIE KWOLEK

7

```
      ¹F I R S T
²P E D A L
      ³O R I G I N A L
⁴S C A T T E R   ⁵E N C L O S E
⁶M O I S T E N
      ⁷C R E A T E
⁸W A S T E
      ⁹P R O T E C T
¹⁰C R I T E R I A
      ¹¹R E L E A S E
¹²S W E E P
      ¹³A P P L Y
¹⁴I N V E N T O R
      ¹⁵T R A S H
```

FLORENCE PARPART

8

1. Mass
2. Astronomer
3. Rebut
4. Gather
5. Age
6. Rely
7. Emit
8. Together
9. Born
10. Understand
11. Rare
12. Bind
13. Inward
14. Denser
15. Gravitation
16. Explosive

MARGARET BURBIDGE

9

1. Botanist
2. Award
3. Reject
4. Biologist
5. Assume
6. Report
7. Activity
8. Maize
9. Chromosome
10. Concept
11. Laboratory
12. Inherit
13. Nineteenth
14. Transfer
15. Order
16. Control
17. Kernel

BARBARA MCCLINTOCK

10

1. Joint
2. Observatory
3. Class
4. Electron
5. Lens
6. Youthful
7. Neutron
8. Burst
9. Uniform
10. Rotate
11. Nova
12. Entirely
13. Luminosity
14. Length

JOCELYN BURNELL

11

1. Material
2. Astronomical
3. Ring
4. Image
5. Atmosphere
6. Moon
7. Inspect
8. Tornado
9. Circular
10. Height
11. Eclipse
12. Level
13. Light

MARIA MITCHELL

12

13

1.	animal	creature	organism	(factor)
2.	separate	(semi)	extract	remove
3.	growth	(experiment)	tumor	cancer
4.	(media)	graft	attach	join
5.	(cell)	bud	grow	develop
6.	(medicine)	limb	branch	extension
7.	biol	chem	phys	(rev)
8.	name	identify	(multi)	recognize
9.	discharge	emit	(organism)	release
10.	disperse	spread	strew	(embryo)
11.	prize	(million)	award	tribute
12.	mass	cluster	group	(transplant)
13.	(extra)	discover	find	unearth
14.	(travel)	fiber	thread	string
15.	embryo	fetus	unborn	(basic)
16.	nerve	skin	muscle	(mini)
17.	matter	(brighten)	substance	material
18.	encompass	(anti)	surround	enclose

RITA LEVI - MONTALCINI

14

MARGARET KNIGHT

16

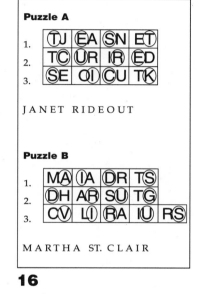

Puzzle A

JANET RIDEOUT

Puzzle B

MARTHA ST. CLAIR

15

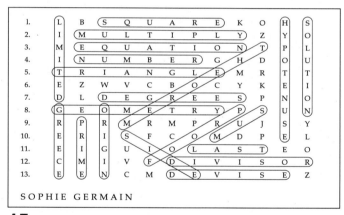

SOPHIE GERMAIN

17

1. Mature
2. Ancient
3. Reptiles
4. Yen
5. Amateur
6. Neck
7. Native
8. Ichthyosaur
9. Natural
10. Geology

MARY ANNING

18

1.	particle	fragment	speck	(semiconductor)
2.	(hypothesis)	question	query	inquiry
3.	bind	(improve)	asten	tie
4.	(reflect)	condense	compress	compact
5.	experiment	(laboratory)	test	trial
6.	(element)	loose	free	unattached
7.	force	energy	(yesterday)	power
8.	gas	liquid	solid	(join)
9.	conductor	(atom)	transmitter	conveyer
10.	research	investigation	study	(computer)
11.	(kinetic)	neutrino	meson	muon
12.	focus	direct	(subatomic)	concentrate
13.	(observatory)	external	outer	exterior
14.	construct	build	(neutrino)	devise

SHIRLEY JACKSON

Women Scientists and Inventors **89**

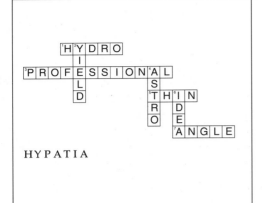

19

HYPATIA

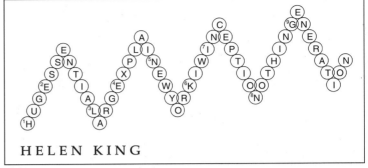

HELEN KING

20

21

D I F F R A C T I O N
P H O T O
R E P E A T E D
C R Y S T A L L O
T E C H N O L O G Y
S E A R C H
Y O U N G
A P P R O A C H
O B J E C T I V E
B L O O D
G R A P H I C
W O R K
I N S U L I N
P E N I C I L L I N

DOROTHY HODGKIN

22

1. Link
2. Aroma
3. Scientist
4. Establish
5. Crystal
6. Benzene
7. Measure
8. Carbon
9. Biological
10. Undergo
11. Hexagon
12. Analysis
13. Diamond
14. Era
15. Medical
16. Refine

KATHLEEN LONSDALE

23

Puzzle A

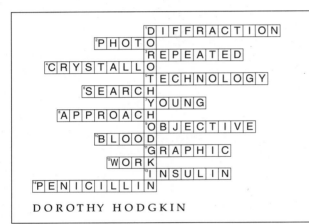

1.
2.
3.

RACHEL BROWN

Puzzle B

1.
2.
3.

ELIZABETH HAZEN

24

1. shell	orbit	path	(helium)
2. atom	(inertia)	molecule	compound
3. theory	(number)	hypothesis	proposition
4. amount	total	sum	(nuclei)
5. (alpha)	completed	filled	occupied
6. model	(sum)	example	plan
7. predict	foretell	(plasma)	prophesy
8. inert	stable	(energy)	fixed
9. common	shared	(freeze)	joint
10. neutron	electron	proton	(nuclear)

MARIA MAYER

25

1. Arrange
2. Lower
3. Individual
4. Central
5. Equip
6. Patent
7. Air
8. Regulate
9. Kind
10. Extend
11. Release

ALICE PARKER

26

```
 1.  F  N  E  L  E  M  E  N  T  S  B
 2.  I  E  G  A  M  M  A  G  T  E  C
 3.  S  U  U  T  X  O  R  A  T  O  R
 4.  S  R  I  M  R  G  B  A  R  E  Z
 5.  I  O  N  I  D  L  Z  R  A  N  N
 6.  O  N  O     E  O  E  C  Y  E  U
 7.  N  S  C     R  D  T  C  U  R  C
 8.     N  E  E  C  O  R  T  A  G  L
 9.  X  B  M  P  R  O  T  O  N  Y  E
10.  E  Y  T  H  E  O  R  Y  X  N  A
11.  B  O  M  B  Z  F  E  R  M  I  R
```

LISE MEITNER

27

1. Cobalt
2. Hypothesis
3. Identical
4. Exhibit
5. Nucleus
6. Symmetry
7. Half
8. Imaginary
9. Unchanged
10. Nobel
11. General
12. Whole
13. Unify

CHIEN-SHIUNG WU

28

```
 G A R B L E
 E
 A C C U R A T E
 C O
 H M
   P
   I
   L
   E A C H
   R E
     A
   O P E R A T E
     R
   P O W E R
     G
 E R R O R
 A     A
 M     M
```

GRACE HOPPER

29

1. PH EH AN SR IE
2. EC TE TP HA EL EI DA
3. VS IT AT RT

HENRIETTA LEAVITT

30

1. Visual
2. Aerial
3. Landsat
4. Environment
5. Resource
6. Illusion
7. Eye
8. Transmit
9. High
10. Optical
11. Mirror
12. Automatic
13. Satellite

VALERIE THOMAS

31

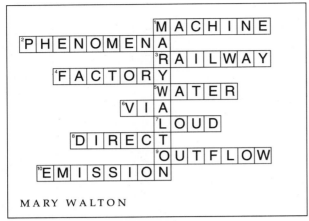

								¹M	A	C	H	I	N	E
²P	H	E	N	O	M	E	N	A						
						³R	A	I	L	W	A	Y		
⁴F	A	C	T	O	R	Y								
					⁵W	A	T	E	R					
				⁶V	I	A								
						⁷L	O	U	D					
⁸D	I	R	E	C	T									
							⁹O	U	T	F	L	O	W	
¹⁰E	M	I	S	S	I	O	N							

MARY WALTON

32

1. Mechanism
2. Agent
3. Relate
4. Yield
5. Simplify
6. Oblique
7. Magnetism
8. Example
9. Refer
10. Verify
11. Interpret
12. Life
13. Law
14. Electricity

MARY SOMERVILLE

33

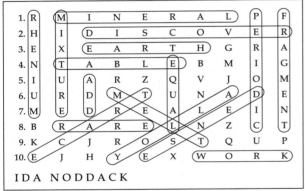

1.	R	M	I	N	E	R	A	L	P	F
2.	H	I	D	I	S	C	O	V	E	R
3.	E	X	E	A	R	T	H	G	R	A
4.	N	T	A	B	L	E	B	M	I	G
5.	I	U	U	R	Z	Q	V	J	O	M
6.	U	R	A	D	M	T	U	N	A	E
7.	M	E	D	D	R	E	E	L	D	N
8.	B	R	A	R	E	L	N	Z	I	T
9.	K	C	J	R	O	S	T	Q	C	P
10.	E	J	H	Y	E	X	W	O	R	K

IDA NODDACK

34

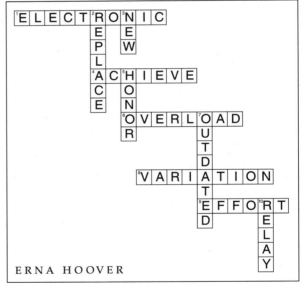

¹E	L	E	C	T	²R	O	³N	I	C
					E		E		
					P		W		
					L				
⁴A	⁵C	H	I	E	V	E			
	O				A				
	N				⁶O	V	E	R	L	O	A	D

ⁱ⁰R E L A Y (vertical)

⁷O U T D A T E D (vertical)

⁸V A R I A T I O N

⁹E F F O R T

ERNA HOOVER

35

1. Fluid
2. Lymph
3. Organism
4. Researcher
5. Extension
6. Nourish
7. Capillaries
8. Excess
9. Substance
10. Attack
11. Body
12. Information
13. Network

FLORENCE SABIN

36

1.
2.
3.

SONYA KOVALEVSKY

37

1.	include	(nucleus)	contain	comprise
2.	rod	stick	(egg)	shaft
3.	arm	(trait)	leg	face
4.	offspring	children	(twenty)	progeny
5.	liver	heart	lung	(ingest)
6.	split	divide	partition	(emerge)
7.	examine	inspect	(sex)	scrutinize
8.	acquire	get	receive	(transmit)
9.	(essential)	specific	particular	distinct
10.	rebut	disprove	(verify)	controvert
11.	latent	hidden	(evident)	dormant
12.	(notice)	regular	average	usual
13.	unite	(sperm)	fuse	combine

NETTIE STEVENS

38

1. Branch
2. Surface
3. Divider
4. Current
5. Fresh
6. Area
7. Formula
8. Display
9. Rear
10. Conduct
11. Two
12. Motion

HERTHA AYRTON

39

1. Radioisotope
2. Organ
3. Sample
4. Antibody
5. Launch
6. Yawning
7. Nitrogen
8. Young
9. Analyze
10. Locate
11. Originate
12. Wide

ROSALYN YALOW

40

```
                    ¹S U B M A R I N E
          ²S E A
                    ³R E S P O N S E
          ⁴D I L E M M A
                    ⁵H U L L
          ⁶A R M
                    ⁷A D A P T
          ⁸B U I L T
                    ⁹H U M A N
       ¹⁰T E L E S C O P E
                    ¹¹R E C O R D
```

SARAH MATHER

41

1.	A	L	U	M	I	N	U	M	G	X	Y	C
2.	R	E	H	B	O	M	B	A	R	D	L	D
3.	T	N	P	E	J	I	S	O	T	O	P	E
4.	I	E	Z	E	L	E	M	E	N	T	T	R
5.	F	R	R	G	E	I	P	Y	M	C	G	P
6.	I	G	I	M	K	J	U	D	G	E	I	H
7.	C	Y	I	S	A	K	M	Q	L	I	O	O
8.	I	T	H	L	O	L	B	W	U	G	S	S
9.	A	O	P	A	R	T	I	C	L	E	O	P
10.	L	H	N	I	T	R	O	G	E	N	L	H
11.	A	Z	Y	M	C	H	E	M	I	S	A	O
12.	J	V	B	C	R	E	A	T	E	Z	T	R
13.	L	D	U	O	X	N	U	C	L	E	I	U
14.	M	F	D	P	R	O	D	U	C	E	O	S
15.	G	R	A	D	I	O	A	C	T	I	V	E
16.	P	T	R	M	A	G	N	E	S	I	U	M

IRENE JOLIOT CURIE

42

1. Glucose
2. Enzymes
3. Respiration
4. Transport
5. Yell
6. Convert
7. Ordinary
8. Reaction
9. Impact

GERTY CORI

SELECTED BIBLIOGRAPHY

Books

Dash, Joan. *The Triumph of Discovery: Women Scientists Who Won the Nobel Prize.* Englewood Cliffs: Julian Messner, 1991. (Rita Levi-Montalcini, Maria Mayer, Barbara McClintock, Rosalyn Yalow)

Grinstein, Louise S, and Paul J. Campbell, eds. *Women of Mathematics.* Westport, CT: Greenwood Press, 1987. (Ada Byron, Sophie Germain, Grace Hopper, Hypatia, Sonya Kovalevsky, Emmy Noether, Mary Somerville)

Hayden, Robert C. *Nine African-American Inventors.* New York: Twenty-First Century Books, 1992. (Alice Parker, Valerie Thomas)

Hayden, Robert C. *Seven African-American Scientists.* New York: Twenty-First Century Books, 1992. (Shirley Jackson)

Levin, Beatrice. *Women and Medicine.* Lincoln, Nebraska: Media Publishing, 1988. (Gerty Cori, Lise Meitner, Rita Levi-Montalcini, Barbara McClintock, Florence Sabin, Helen Taussig)

Macdonald, Anne L. *Feminine Ingenuity.* New York: Ballantine, 1992. (Rachel Brown, Gertrude Elion, Elizabeth Hazen, Erna Hoover, Margaret Knight, Stephanie Kwolek, Sarah Mather, Florence Parpart, Janet Rideout, Martha St. Clair, Mary Walton)

Biographical Dictionaries

McMurray, Emily J., ed. *Notable Twentieth-Century Scientists.* Detroit: Gale Research, Inc., 1995. (Shirley Jackson, Rosalyn Yalow)

Millar, David, Ian Millar, John Millar, and Margaret Millar. *Chambers Concise Dictionary of Scientists.* Cambridge, England: W & R Chambers, Ltd., 1989. (Jocelyn Burnell, Kathleen Lonsdale, Ida Noddack, Chien-shiung Wu)

Ogilvie, Marilyn Bailey. *Women in Science: Antiquity Through the Nineteenth Century.* Cambridge, MA: The MIT Press, 1993. (Mary Anning, Hertha Ayrton, Ada Byron, Marie Curie, Sophie Germain, Hypatia, Helen King, Margaret Knight, Sonya Kovalevsky, Henrietta Leavitt, Maria Mitchell, Emmy Noether, Florence Sabin, Mary Somerville, Nettie Stevens)

General Biographical Guides

Weisbard, Phyllis Holman, Rima D. Apple, and Susan E. Searing, eds. *The History of Women and Science, Health, and Technology.* Madison, WI: University of Wisconsin System Women's Studies Librarian, 1993. (Bibliographic guide to sources of information about numerous women in science and mathematics)

Encyclopedias

Encyclopedia Britannica. 15th ed. 1995. (Margaret Burbidge, Gerty Cori, Gertrude Elion, Rosalind Franklin, Irene Joliot-Curie, Henrietta Leavitt, Rita Levi-Montalcini, Kathleen Lonsdale, Lise Meitner, Maria Mitchell, Chien-shiung Wu, Rosalyn Yalow. *Also see* Conservation of energy, Antony Hewish, William Fowler.)

Compton's Interactive Encyclopedia. Compton's NewMedia, Inc., 1994. (Rosalind Franklin, Dorothy Hodgkin, Sonya Kovalevsky, Maria Mayer, Lise Meitner, Maria Mitchell, Chien-shiung Wu; also see Acquired Immunodeficiency Syndrome, Charles Babbage, Antoine Becquerel, Curie family, Enrico Fermi, Lymphatic System, Nuclear Physics, Pulsar, Radioactivity, Submarine)

The Internet

Augusta Ada Byron, Countess of Lovelace
http://loki.sonoma.edu/Math/faculty/falbo/AdaByron.html

Marie Curie—A Biographical Insight
http://zen.sunderland.ac.uk/~hb5hco/marie.htm

Gertrude Belle Elion
http://web.mit.edu/invent/www/inventorsA-H/elion.html

Rosalind Franklin
http://www.gene.com:80/AE/AB/BC/Rosalind_Franklin.html

Sophie Germain
http://www.scottlan.edu/lriddle/women/germain.htm

Dr. Dorothy Crowfoot Hodgkin: Chemist, Crystallographer, Humanitarian
http://www.almaz.com/nobel/chemistry/dch.html

Erna Schneider Hoover
http://web.mit.edu/invent/www/inventorsA-H/hoover.html

Grace Hopper
http://web.mit.edu/invent/www/inventorsA-H/hopper.html

Hypatia
http://www.scottlan.edu/lriddle/women/hypatia.htm

Shirley Ann Jackson: Physicist (Theoretical)
http://indigo.lib.lsu.edu/lib/chem/display/jackson.html

Irene Joliot-Curie
http://www.netsrq.com:80/~dbois/joliot.html

Industrial History Includes Women Inventors: The Woman Edison (Margaret Knight)
http://web.mit.edu/invent/www/inventorsR-Z/whm2.html

Sofia Kovalevskaya (Sonya Kovalevsky)
http://www-groups.dcs.st-and.ac.uk/~history/Mathematicians/Kovalevskaya.html

Kevlar, the Wonder Fiber (Stephanie Kwolek)
http://web.mit.edu/invent/www/inventorsI-Q/kwolek.html

The Henrietta Leavitt Flat Screen Space Theater
http://www.voicenet.com/~peterscc

Kathleen Yardley Lonsdale
http://www.physics.ucla.edu/~cwp/Phase2/Lonsdale,_Kathleen_Yardley@8480138866.html

Maria Goeppert Mayer Papers
http://orpheus.ucsd.edu:80/speccoll/testing/html/mss0020d.html

Barbara McClintock
http://zodiac.zoo.utoronto.ca:80/~dgwynne/plorch/wis/bm-1.html

Lise Meitner
http://www.sph.umich.edu:80/~bbusby/meitner.htm

Emmy Amalie Noether
http://www-groups.dcs.st-and.ac.uk/%7Ehistory/Mathematicians/Noether_Emmy.html

Nettie Maria Stevens
http://www.mbl.edu:80/html/WOMEN/stevens.html

Valerie L. Thomas Retires
http://nssdc.gsfc.nasa.gov/nssdc_news/sept95/04_j_green_0995.html

Mary Walton
http://web.mit.edu/invent/www/inventorsR-Z/walton.html

Dr. Chien-shiung Wu
http://www.witi.org:80/Center/Museum/Hall/Inductees/dwu.html